HOW TO ANNIHILATE A NARCISSIST IN THE FAMILY COURT

HOW TO ANNIHILATE A NARCISSIST IN THE FAMILY COURT

Rachel Watson

A detailed guide on how to expose a cruel narcissist's true character

To my husband and my three boys, who are, and always will be, one step ahead!

CONTENTS

INTRODUCTION

Going to court against a narcissist can be a heart-breaking and soul-destroying experience. It can lead to years of extraordinary stress for you, any future spouse, and your extended family. Court proceedings can have devastating effects on the children involved too.

If you have no option but to enter court proceedings, then you are at the right place. I will arm you with the ammunition required, to assist you on your litigation journey against the narcissist. He has his mask firmly in place on entering the courtroom — his empathetic and caring mask. Your mission is to expose the narcissist's hidden, ugly face beneath, and, reveal your true character, not the character the narcissist will portray you to be. The more prepared you are, the more chance you will have of being successful in your endeavours.

The narcissist is at his best in the courtroom. He thrives on the entire experience. It's showtime for the narcissist. He is in his element, and he will be rubbing his hands in glee at the prospects of the control he can hold over you by way of court orders. The court orders may benefit you, but the court orders can also be restrictive for you, the empath parent. Along the journey, you will, at times, struggle and feel defeated.

The narcissist is an extremely powerful opponent in the courtroom and taking him on in the battle, is a brave and difficult task. A narcissist will go to shocking extremes to torment you and 'win'. I will teach you how to use every situation to your advantage. Know that the narcissist never wins. Even when he thinks he has won.

With the knowledge, I am going to give you, and your battle armour intact, you will be ready to conquer. He will not know what has hit him. You can do this!

LEGAL DISCLAIMER

I must make it clear; I am not a solicitor or an advocate and have had no formal legal training. My advice to you is based purely on my own twelve-year experience with a narcissistic abuser. I defended myself against and raised, legal action in the Court of Session, the highest civil court in Scotland. I was successful in my outcomes. I have had some representation at times, but most of the time, I represented myself.

I will focus on proceedings primarily in the civil court in Scotland, which have many similarities to those in England, Ireland and Wales. However, proceedings will be different in other courts and of course, other countries.

I cannot guarantee you will be successful in your court proceedings. I cannot give you guarantees about contact or residence orders in your circumstances. If you have not already sought legal representation or advice, then I strongly suggest you do so. If you are representing yourself in court, then I suggest you obtain some basic legal advice to assist you along the way.

The principles I will teach you shall apply to litigation against a narcissist in any courtroom. The examples I shall show you are from my own experience only.

Narcissists can be male or female but for the purpose of this book, and since it relates to my own experience, I shall refer to the narcissist as a 'he'. I shall also refer to the 'child', but the same advice applies if you have more than one child.

1. THE HEALING PROCESS

So, where do we start?

For all victims of narcissistic abuse, a period of healing is required. You may not have time to heal before the commencement of your litigation, but if you do have time, then you need to try to heal yourself as much as possible before you start the litigation process. Court hearings can be months apart, so take the time in between hearings to heal your body and your mind and keep yourself grounded. The length of time it takes to heal can vary from one person to another, depending on what you have experienced. Some victims may never heal. I believe it is an ongoing process; you must refresh your memory over time, of the healing principles you learn, to stay focused.

You will no doubt have been through a tumultuous time. If you have recently separated from the narcissist, you may be feeling depressed, weak, angry and frustrated. You may wish to seek revenge for all that he has done to you and your family, but feel that you are not a vindictive person, and therefore he continues to 'get away with it'. You might feel lost; you have lost your self-esteem and self-confidence, you feel as if he has stolen your personality, and you don't know who you are anymore. You may feel confused as to why, others around him, don't see what you see. You may fear your narcissist.

In my situation, I had all these feelings. My narcissist, my husband and father of our child, was violent. He was controlling, manipulating, convincing and scary. I feared for my life, and I fled in the middle of the night, from our home in Dubai. (As detailed in my memoir, 'The Narcissist's Bait').

A few weeks later, I returned to my parents' home in Scotland with my ten-month-old son. I was distraught, frightened and physically and emotionally, drained. Within two days the police were at my door followed by an officer of the court, serving me a summons to appear at The Court of Session in Edinburgh. The narcissist had started legal action against me for the criminal offence of child abduction. I was astounded! I had told him I was travelling to Scotland; he knew I was a kind and caring mother who would never try to stop him having a relationship with his child. He treated me like a criminal while he played the victim to everyone concerned.

It was the beginning of my twelve-year litigation nightmare. The narcissist had lost control of me in the household and was now going to attempt to control me through the court system.

I didn't have time to heal before court proceedings started, but I learned to heal myself along the way. If you are feeling some or all the feelings, I have described above; then you are not currently in an emotionally stable frame of mind – your narcissist has rendered you into this state. He has no doubt belittled, manipulated and scared you into a person you no longer recognise. The emotional condition you are in now is going to be a huge advantage to the narcissist in the courtroom for reasons I shall explain to you in later chapters. Do not be mistaken into thinking the judge will see a victim before his eyes, feel sorry for you and give you all that you ask. Your first lesson!

If you feel as I have described, and litigation is imminent, then I strongly suggest you get legal representation to handle matters for you, at least in the early stages. You can always go on to represent yourself at a later stage. The decisions taken in the initial phase of court proceedings are going to be the most important ones (about who the child lives with and how much time the child spends with the other parent, and, about protection orders). You will understand why I offer this advice as you read on.

So, what do I mean by healing? We all heal in different ways. The aim is to get yourself back to being you. The person you were before you met the narcissist. The result, however, will be that you emerge a stronger, wiser version of you. The trauma you have gone through with the narcissist has taught you lessons in life you don't even realise. You will now have an urge to understand what the narcissist is and why he has done this to you, and your child.

Understanding this will be the key to your healing path. The more you understand about the narcissist and his core beliefs and values, and, the more you understand about his behaviour, the stronger and more powerful you become. Understanding who he is and why he does what he does will be a huge advantage to you in the courtroom and, when dealing with the professionals, you are going to face in your litigation journey.

Methods of healing vary from person to person. Some choose a religious path; some choose a spiritual path; some immerse themselves in sport. I think I tried a bit of everything! It helps to understand what attracted the narcissist to you in the first place, and this will most certainly go back to your childhood. Healing childhood wounds is a good place to start.

The first book I read on my healing journey was 'Forgiveness' by Iyanla Vanzant. Now before you think to yourself;

 'What on earth is she talking about, I'm not ready to forgive that loser!'

I hear you. I was not ready to forgive him, either. But the lessons the book taught me were fundamental to the healing process. By forgiving, you are not saying that you are agreeing with or condoning the narcissist's behaviour, you are choosing to let go and learning to understand that everything happens for a reason. Everything is the way it is meant to be, at this moment in time. You forgive so you can free your mind, and this will allow you to open yourself, to wholeheartedly love in the future. When you fall in love again, it will be the real deal. Even if, after you finish reading the book, you have not forgiven the narcissist, you will have forgiven yourself, and possibly significant family members in your life. This forgiveness will be hugely rewarding in your years to come. You do not want to remain sad, bitter, confused and angry. These emotions are going to ooze out of you in the courtroom and in front of the professionals you come across in the process. (Solicitors, advocates, mediators and child welfare reporters).

If you remain that person, the narcissist has won. Do not let the narcissist defeat you at the first step. Free your mind using whatever method you choose. Try various methods until one feels right for you and you find a method that you enjoy.

You may choose to go to a therapist or psychologist. If you do, then find one with experience of dealing with emotional or physical abuse, and, personality disorders. Yoga, Pilates, or sport of your choice can help the healing process. Your body needs to be strong as well as your mind. You need to feel good about yourself again. I found myself going down a more spiritual path, and I did both yoga and Pilates. It helped!

Other books I read on my healing journey were 'The Power of Now' and 'A New Earth' by Eckhart Tolle and 'The Healing Self' and 'The Seven Spiritual Laws of Success' by Deepak Chopra. The latter, I still refer to today. More recently, I have read 'Why Does He Do That?' by Lundy Bancroft. The knowledge these books gave me was so valuable and has benefited many other areas of my life. Relationships in work, relationships with family members and relationships with my children, have all been affected positively. These books helped me grow as a person, and this, in turn, allowed me to present myself in a better light during my litigation process in later years.

I studied narcissistic behaviour like I was studying for a master's degree. I watched countless videos on YouTube, relating to narcissism. I read articles, blogs and books, whatever I could find. I will talk more about narcissistic behaviour in a later chapter. Studying their behaviour is not only important in the healing process; it is fundamental in the litigation process.

Another part of my healing journey was dealing with stress. My mind raced at night. I couldn't sleep well, with all that was going on. The narcissist still managed to consume my thoughts daily. I had had enough. Three years after I left the narcissist and divorced him, I rekindled the relationship with my first ever love. We were at college together. I wanted to give my all to my new relationship. I did not want to think about the narcissistic ex twenty-four hours a day. I wanted to concentrate on my child at the time and later, my three children. I had to get the narcissist out of my head. I started to watch meditation videos to help me sleep. Again, I found these on YouTube. They worked a treat! They helped me to clear my mind, and, along with the books I was reading, helped to slow down my thoughts and enabled me to stop worrying so much. One morning I woke up in the early hours with my entire body vibrating. I had no idea what it meant at the time, but whatever had happened, it was significant in my healing process. I turned over and said to my husband;

'That's it; I feel healed! I feel awakened. Cured!'

I desperately googled healing and vibrations, and this took me down a whole other learning path of chakras and spiritual healing. I did not delve much further, but it certainly awakened something inside me and gave me a huge boost. I downloaded a horoscope app on my phone, (Astrolis.com) and I couldn't believe how in tune with my thoughts and daily activities it seemed to be. I still check it daily for guidance!

I strongly believe that had I healed earlier, then I would not have gone through the same level of stress that I did throughout the twelve-year court process. I would not have put my husband, extended family and children, through similar amounts of stress. I would not have allowed the narcissist to affect me and my behaviour to the extent he did.

Healing allows you to move on with your life, free from the control that the narcissist subjects you to. You will never be truly free from his power until you let go of all the negative feelings the narcissist has planted in you. Once your mind is free and clear, your body is stronger, and you have found your sense of self, you arm yourself with your first weapon in the war against the narcissist in the courtroom. **Emotional stability.**

2. CIVIL FAMILY COURT

Most separated families in Scotland manage to agree on contact arrangements themselves. Arrangements can then be formalised legally if so wished. If you have a child and have separated from a narcissist, however, matters will likely end up having to be resolved by the civil courts. It's important to understand the reality of the difficulties in going to court against a narcissistic opponent.

There is a huge variance in the length of time a contact dispute can go on for in the Scottish court system due to the complexities of individual circumstances. Many contact disputes in the Sheriff court will resolve within six to twelve months. Some less and on some occasions, it will go into years. When you go up against a narcissist, however, be prepared to be in it for the long haul.

My case went on for twelve years in the Court of Session. I am without a doubt that the fundamental reason it went on for so many years, was the narcissist's need for control and his unwillingness to 'reason' and 'compromise' in matters affecting our child. One hearing would become five hearings, due to his ability to deceive, manipulate and convince.

Narcissists love the attention court hearings bring. They may find loopholes in the law to cause delays, raise unnecessary legal actions to torment you, appeal judges' decisions to frustrate you, and do so with the best lawyers they can afford if given the opportunity. They will attempt to 'drain' you, emotionally and financially, hoping that you will give in and submit. It can cause you, the empath, extraordinary stress.

Court proceedings can, in some cases, be detrimental to your health. It can cause sleepless nights, affect your concentration at work, cause physical skin problems such as rashes, lead to substance abuse and lead to depression, even suicidal thoughts. Legal action can cause feelings of anxiousness, guilt, frustration and pressure. And that's without the added distress caused by a narcissistic opponent.

Legal proceedings can upset your day to day life enormously. You may find yourself entrenched with sudden, unexpected financial demands which appear to be never-ending. You may face the painful experience of having to sell your assets such as your car or your property, purely to pay huge legal bills. You may have to take loans, causing money worries for years ahead. You may have to miss work regularly to attend court hearings.

The whole process can be devastatingly difficult on you and those closest to you, particularly the child involved.

You may find yourself in courtroom disputes with the narcissist until your child becomes a young adult.

Teenagers like to make decisions about matters which involve them. The Scottish courts listen to the child's voice from an early age, and I believe this is of great benefit to the empath parent. The narcissist finds it extremely difficult to relinquish 'control' over the empath and the child. He will continue to fight until the bitter end to hold onto whatever control he can.

I say 'fight' because when the narcissist and the empath go to court against each other, they go to court as enemies. The focus is on 'winning' and getting 'justice'. The empath wants to prove they are a good, law-abiding citizen and prove that the narcissist is the opposite. With a narcissist, it is not just a battle you are heading into; it's a war. The narcissist feels they must emerge victorious at all costs. You, the empath, tend to progress in life, through reasoning, understanding and compromising with people.

The narcissist gets what he wants in life through charming, persuasion, manipulation and aggression. You've given up trying to come to an amicable agreement with this despicable human being. You've given up on waiting for karma to get him. Fighting him in court sometimes feels like the only option left, whether you are defending yourself against, or, initiating court action.

Now put yourself in the judge's position. They are not here to referee battles between two enemies and to declare one party victorious in their war. They don't want to see antagonistic or confrontational behaviour by either party. The judge, in the civil family court, must determine the best solution for the child in the unfortunate circumstances in which the parents have separated. The judge is looking to find shared outlooks and common goals. The judge takes a peace-making and compromising approach to matters. The judge's focus is on resolving the contact dispute to the child's benefit and bringing about meaningful change to the lives of those involved.

So, while it may be a war you are going into, in your mind, you must remain fully conscious throughout the process of what is going through the *Judge's* mind.

It can, therefore, be beneficial to **gain a basic understanding of how civil family court works and gain an understanding of the role of the judge.**

Look at family law solicitors' websites in your country, which can give you a good idea of what to expect regarding divorce, and the child's living and contact arrangements thereafter. Learn the meaning of some courtroom terminology. (For example, pursuer, defendant, writ, affidavit, proof hearing). Study the website of the Child Reporting Agency, which applies to the country in which you are living. These websites will all give you vital information on what to expect throughout court proceedings. (See Resources chapter).

The more you understand about the legal side of things, the more comfortable you will feel about entering litigation. You might expect to go to court, be in there for two hours, and come out with a decision and have that matter behind you. Regrettably, the reality is, you could go to court, be in there for five minutes, have another hearing scheduled for two months, be in there for two hours, have another hearing scheduled for two months and then get the decision.

Court proceedings can take twists and turns you would never imagine. Once you start to learn the process, it can reduce the levels of stress, as you will come to know what to expect. If you have solicitors, ask questions, get a clear picture of what is likely to happen at the next hearing, to avoid disappointment.

You might want to start representing yourself one day. By watching closely to the way court procedures operate, studying the particular court's website, and learning as much as you can from publications, you may, like me, think to yourself; 'I can do this!'

In Scotland, civil family court proceedings take place in the Sheriff Court or the Court of Session.

A judge in Scotland will take a child's views on matters and determine what 'weight' the child's views should get depending on their competency. (For example; Is the child mature enough? Is the child intelligent and fully aware of the circumstances? Is the child displaying signs of being coached by a parent?) Judges can use welfare reporters to obtain the child's views; they can use a form which is sent to the child and completed independently (possibly with a teacher). On some occasions, the judge will speak to the child in private. The child does not simply get to 'decide' themselves at a certain age before becoming an adult; the judge will always make the final decision.

In my situation, the judge spoke to my son for the first time around the age of eight and, took his views into account. He later spoke to him around the age of twelve, and on this occasion, gave 'significant weight' to my son's views on matters.

Court representation can get very costly if you don't qualify for Legal Aid, particularly in the Court of Session. Cases in this court generally require a solicitor and an advocate representing you. The cost of solicitors and advocates vary enormously. You may have no option but to represent yourself or risk losing your entire life savings.

Even when you represent yourself, you still need to pay court fees and can be instructed by the judge to pay for costly welfare reports.

You may be lucky and get awarded 'expenses' by the judge. (The other party is ordered to pay some or all of the costs back to you). With a narcissist, however, it may just be the start of another battle in which you seek payment.

 Research legal costs in your area/court so you can prepare accordingly.

When facing lengthy litigation proceedings regularly, some matters with the narcissist may be worth 'letting go of' rather than putting yourself through the financial burden and stress. Don't see it as the narcissist winning. **Pick and choose your battles wisely** to do what is best for you and your family.

3. COURT ORDERS

When family's breakdown and separate, the civil courts in Scotland hope that they can assist in resolving matters without the need for court orders, so far as possible. Solicitors will attempt to broker an agreement, on behalf of the parties. Or, you and the narcissist may attempt to broker your agreement. The ideal outcome for the judge is that if he should have to make an order, it is on an already agreed solution. However, as you know, with a narcissist, its is difficult to agree on all matters, and therefore the judge must often be the one to 'decide' and impose his decision, through a court order.

Judges use several orders to determine where the child will live and how contact will take place with other family members (residence orders and contact orders, sometimes referred to as custody and access). There are several protection orders available (for example exclusion orders, interdicts & non-harassment orders).

For example;

Residence order: orders with whom the child shall live. (The resident parent)

Interdict: prevents a parent from carrying out certain actions or going certain places, for example, prevents a parent removing the child from the care and control of the resident parent, or from removing the child out of the jurisdiction of the court.

Compulsory supervision order: ordering the local authorities to be responsible for looking after and helping the child

Contact order: orders detailing dates, times and specifics of contact between the non-resident parent and the child

Specific issue order: an order for a particular reason for example;

- Orders that contact with the non-resident parent must take place in a child contact centre.

- Orders that the non-resident parent must submit their passport to a solicitor during contact.

- Orders that the resident parent must keep the non-resident parent updated on the child's health, education and general wellbeing.

THE BENEFITS OF COURT ORDERS

Court orders are beneficial to the empath and protect you and the child from the narcissist's difficult behaviour. When you have a contact order, it's a blessing to know that the dates are specific and that the other party is breaking the law if they do not follow them. Orders minimise disruptions, since you know in advance, exactly when and where the contact will take place. It reduces arguments between the empath and the narcissist since it limits the need for discussion on arrangements. Some narcissists like the structure and the ability to plan out their contact time hour by hour.

If you fear your narcissist, you will need protection, and you can get this by way of orders if they are deemed necessary. By law, violent men are still entitled to have contact with their children. They still have parental rights and responsibilities. Very early on, I realised it would be of no benefit to me to try to prevent contact between my son and his father, and that I should allow the child to love his father and form a relationship with him.

Courts are very unlikely to stop a father having contact with a child because the mother 'worries he might harm the child'. There must be evidence that the child is in danger. Many narcissists will appear to adore their child, but many empaths worry that the violent narcissist will do something to the child to punish the empath for leaving him. In my personal experience, these fears eased over time but never disappeared completely. If you have this fear, then follow the advice in later chapters, regarding communication and evidence and request protection orders that would suit your circumstances.

Having a court order in place has the benefit that the narcissist's behaviour is going to be monitored and will be under scrutiny by a judge. He very quickly learns he has to tame his behaviour, to avert the attention of the judge. This scrutiny can give you a huge amount of protection. The narcissist is now going to change tack and play the role of the best parent in the world.

CONTACT ORDERS -WHAT CAN GO WRONG?

YOUR BEHAVIOUR

On coming out of the relationship with the violent narcissist, it can be excruciatingly difficult for the empath parent to accept that they must send someone so precious, their child, to spend time with a person they find so despicable and often, dangerous. It can be heart-breaking. Once you have healed, however, it becomes easier to accept and understand.

The empath parent's behaviour is also going to be under the scrutiny of the judge for as long as there is a contact order in place. This scrutiny can be challenging for the empath parent when the narcissist is on a mission to torment you and continue to abuse you through the court system. If the empath parent's behaviour ever slips, the narcissist will be straight to the court to blow it all out of proportion and paint the empath parent in a bad light. The narcissist will embellish his version of events in efforts to gain the judge's sympathy.

However, by following the advice herewith, the narcissist won't get that opportunity!

VARIATIONS TO ORDERS

The main difficulty with contact orders is, over the years, they need to change and must adapt to various circumstances. Narcissists use every one of these opportunities to try to paint themselves as the best parent in the world, and you, the empath as the worst. Unless the change benefits the narcissist, they will object to it and fight against it. Typically, it ends up going back to court since there is no such word as 'compromise' in the narcissist's dictionary.

For example;

- The order may need to be varied if you wish to move to a new house and therefore, school.

- It may need to change if the narcissist breaches an order or disrupts contact and you feel that the order needs to be more specific.

- The contact order may need to adapt to the child's age. As the child gets older, they may want to have some say in matters which affect them.

- The child may get distressed during contact and ask to reduce or cease the contact with the narcissistic parent.

Things come up, and sometimes imminent contact arrangements must change at the last minute due to unforeseen circumstances. The narcissistic parent will use these situations to try to frustrate you and exert his control. I will teach you how to mitigate his disruptive behaviour.

COURT ORDER COMPLIANCE

It is important to comply with court orders; if you fail to do this, you will be breaking the law. The narcissist will use this as ammunition against you forever after. The narcissist is *waiting* for you to break the law! Don't ever give him the satisfaction. If you feel that you are unable to comply with the contact order any longer, then make arrangements to go to the court to explain why and get the order varied.

If you find yourself in a situation of force majeure (for example you were driving to handover the child for contact, and the car broke down) then document what happened, try to make other arrangements, try to have a witness to events, and the judge will, of course, understand that from time to time, these things happen. Be careful how you communicate to the narcissist in such circumstances, stick to facts and don't get emotional.

The narcissist, will, on the other hand, fail to comply with court orders, particularly contact orders. He won't be able to keep the mask firmly in place for all those years! You can use this to your advantage. The narcissist will disrupt the contact, show up late, drop the child off late, especially if they know you have plans and need the contact to be timely. They will breach orders regarding payments to the empath parent. They will even obstruct *their* contact, in an attempt to make it look like *you* caused the obstruction. The narcissist is oblivious to any suffering caused to the child.

If the narcissist fails to comply with a court order, it is then up to you to decide if you want to go back to court and ask the judge to do something about it. You want to see the narcissist punished for his disruptive behaviour and you want to prevent it from happening in the future. Remind yourself of what the judge is thinking. The process is going to cause you and your family stress and cost you financially.

What may feel like a fundamental breach to *you* may not be considered so by the judge. There may be no repercussions for his behaviour since the narcissist is extremely talented at talking his way out of things. He can be very convincing. The empath parent is left extremely frustrated and feeling like the narcissist has got away with it once again.

Each time you go to court, it will have a detrimental effect on the child. Children sense stress and overhear things. Weigh up the pros and cons and decide if it is worth it in the bigger scheme of things. Do not worry; you are going to learn how to expose the narcissist and show the judge which one of you is the obstructive character.

UNILATERAL DECISIONS

Understand the meaning of 'unilateral decisions'. Do not make unilateral decisions if the narcissist has 'parental rights and responsibilities', which he will do if his name is on the child's birth certificate. Parents with parental rights and responsibilities are entitled to consultation, regarding the child's upbringing (health, education & welfare). The judge will look poorly on you if you exclude the narcissist from these discussions.

I know it is almost impossible to get a narcissistic parent to agree mutually, and this is going to test your strength of character. You must try your best to adhere to this, though.

Here are a few examples of what NOT to do, behind the narcissist parent's back;

- Christen the child in your chosen religion

- Change the child's name

- Change the child's school

- Move the child to a different city or country

- Fail to inform the other parent if the child has a hospital emergency or requires non-routine medical attention

If you do take a unilateral decision, and you feel there is no other option, then be prepared to explain the reason as to why it was in the child's best interests to do so and have proof of your attempts to consult and come to an agreement on the matter with the narcissistic parent.

Judges take the matter of unilateral decisions seriously, and it can result in a black mark against you if your reasonable explanation isn't good enough. The narcissist may accuse you of alienating the child, and your behaviour will be under the spotlight. You are handing ammunition to the narcissist for future court hearings.

If you take important unilateral decisions, you may find that you will then get more specific 'orders' directed towards you. The more orders directed towards you can make you look like you are an obstructive parent. If you are uncertain whether to do something or not, then take legal advice.

UNNECESSARY ORDERS
The narcissist loves requesting the judge to order you to do something and for the judge to grant that order. The narcissist feels powerful and feels like he has 'won' in these circumstances. The power and control are what the narcissist feeds on.

Therefore, the narcissist will try to convince the judge to order you to do something that you feel is not necessary. **A judge only makes orders if they deem that there is a need for that order to be in place.** The order can taint your character if, there was no reason for the order to be made, it is in place purely because of the narcissists controlling nature. It can be extremely frustrating if this happens. You can see the situation clearly, but the judge can't.

For example, you may update the narcissist on the telephone regularly, with regards to the child's wellbeing.

The narcissist may claim to the court that you don't keep him updated on the child's wellbeing and you never have done. He is going to attempt to gain sympathy from the court. He will portray himself as the poor father, alienated from his child, by the evil mother. He will do this in any way he can and go to despicable extremes in his efforts to portray you as a terrible parent. He will lie. He may even falsify evidence.

The judge may believe the narcissist's false allegations since it's his word against yours since you updated him on the telephone, you have no proof. The narcissist is extremely convincing. The judge may 'order' you to keep the narcissist updated on the child's health, education and wellbeing.

You are left shocked; you did not expect the narcissist to stoop to such a level as to lie blatantly to the judge.

This court order is detrimental to you since it 'appears' that you could be an obstructive or alienating parent who withheld this information. Withholding information from the narcissistic parent is serious ammunition for him. And now he has the proof.

The narcissist wins this battle. The narcissist does not care if you update him or not on the child's wellbeing. The child is used simply as a pawn.

Typical claims from a narcissist;

- 'She won't let me see him.'

- 'She won't let me speak to him.'

- 'She makes contact difficult for us.'

- 'She doesn't allow me to speak to his school.'

- 'She doesn't tell me about medical problems.'

So, what can you do? I will teach you, in later chapters, how to prevent this. You can predict the narcissist is going to do this, and therefore, you will be firmly one step ahead. Through evidence, and changing the way you communicate with the narcissist, and with the judge, you will not allow the narcissist to win another battle!

4. MAKE A PLAN

If you have not already finalised the child's living situation and contact arrangements with the narcissist and the court, then this is the next step.

You might be lucky and be able to agree with the narcissist on several matters. If you are, then I advise to document it in a 'Parenting Plan', and get it formalised with a solicitor in a 'Minute of Agreement' so that it is legally binding. You can get help on how to make a parenting plan on the Scottish government website. (See 'Resources' chapter at the end).

If you cannot agree with the narcissist on how to co-parent, then the court will make the decisions for you. Therefore, it is vital to decide what you want, understand what the narcissist wants, and attempt to find some common ground. Since the narcissist's world revolves around power and control, it is very unlikely that he will agree to what you request, and matters will end up in front of a judge for a decision to be imposed.

It will help the judge immensely if you have a clear outline of what you seek and the reasons why. If you are seeking to be the resident parent (have the child live with you), then you want to prove to the judge you are responsible and able to cope with the task in hand. Plan how you will manage financially and what help you can get in advance so you can show the judge you are in position and ready.

You probably seek to have the most contact time and to limit the narcissist's contact time. You will no doubt worry about the effects of the narcissist's behaviour on the child. The narcissist is only thinking one thing; 'I have to win this!' Regardless of what it is, he is fighting. In the judge's eyes, co-parenting with an equal amount of parenting time may be viewed as the fair option.

You cannot gain more contact time by telling the judge the child's father is a narcissistic abuser and therefore must spend more time with you, don't fall into that trap!

You probably worry that the narcissistic parent is going to turn the child against you if they have a large amount of contact time together. You may worry about the narcissistic parent's aggressive behaviour in front of the child.

If your narcissist has been abusive in the home and you are concerned about abusive behaviour around the child, then the judge may order that contact take place between the narcissist and the child in a child contact centre. (i.e. supervised contact in a safe, neutral location). These centres are all over Scotland. The judge will need factual evidence of **recent** behaviour; historical behaviour may not hold much weight. The narcissist will certainly fight you on this point. A narcissist cannot face the assumption that their parenting needs monitoring. To be forced into supervised contact by a judge causes such a narcissistic injury (blow to their ego) that some may, at this point, explode into a rage or flee and choose not to have contact at all. Narcissists cannot handle perceived or real criticism of their parenting skills. If they do agree to attend the contact centre, it will not be the end of the matter. The narcissist will then become fixated on getting the judge to agree to unsupervised contact going forward.

Layout the contact arrangements you seek, in writing, and pad it up a bit, so there is some room for negotiation. The judge always likes to make things as fair as possible, so if you can be seen to 'give' a little when it goes to court, then this will go in your favour.

It is important here to concentrate on why it is in the 'child's best interests' to have the contact time that you request, and why it is not in the 'child's best interests' to have the contact requested by the narcissist.

Most narcissists will stoop to low levels to win over the judge and get an order for the child to live with them. The narcissist will do this, even if they have not been active in the child's day to day life. Regrettably, they don't care about what *is* best for the child. They will go to great lengths, however, to 'appear' to care. As discussed earlier, they will be dishonest, and they will make despicable false allegations against you.

They are so skilful in their ability to do this and, come across as the caring, empathetic parent; it will shock you to the core.

If you have already been awarded residency then there is a good chance that somewhere down the line the narcissist will apply for residency to be transferred to them, even when there is a contact order for shared parenting on a 50/50 basis.

If there has been no fundamental change in circumstances, then there would be no good reason for the residency order to be changed, however, if you have denied contact to the narcissist, they may use this as a reason to have residency changed over.

When building your defence for residency, think to yourself, 'Now and in the future, what issue may arise regarding our child's health, education and wellbeing'? 'Why would it be more beneficial for me to remain the resident parent and why would it be less beneficial for my ex to be the resident parent?

For example;

Do you live closer to the school?

Do you work fewer hours than your ex and have more flexibility to go back and forward to school?

Are you the one who will volunteer and help with fundraising efforts at the school?

Are you a member of the school parent council and do you get involved in activities?

If your child is sick, have you been the one who had the flexibility to pick up the child from school at short notice?

Are you the one to take the child to birthday parties and playdates?

Are the child's close friends in your area and do they get together regularly?

Are there any risks to the child's happiness and stability if a change in residency went ahead? If so, state the risks, and the expected effect on the child but be careful not to sound like you are badmouthing the narcissists parenting skills. Stick to facts and keep emotions out of it so far as possible.

Build a positive case in which you sound encouraging and supportive of your ex and your child having meaningful contact with each other and this will counter any efforts of the narcissist to make you appear to be vindictive and bitter or a bad parent.

If you have denied your ex contact, and you are worried that there is good reason that the judge may award the narcissist sole residency, then you could suggest' joint legal residency' if this is applicable in the country in which you live.

The narcissist wants to 'win' so if they see that you are both treated equally in their mind; they may agree on this option. It may be less headache for you to take this option rather than a lengthy court battle.

The way you communicate your plan is significant in this battle. You will learn how to do this in the next chapter, and I will give you an example of how to communicate a request for you to remain the resident parent.

REVERSE PSYCHOLOGY

If a narcissist has a clear understanding of what things are important to you in a contact order, then these are the points he will go against you on. As mentioned previously, he is a powerful opponent, and therefore you are setting yourself up for disappointment on a more trivial matter which could, in some situations, get better dealt with out of court.

So for example, if the child has football in your home town every Saturday, and you want the child to continue to go to the football, during the narcissist's contact weekend, the narcissist is going to say NO! There is a good possibility the judge will agree with the narcissist; he may accept that during the narcissist's contact time, *he* decides what activities they will do, especially if the contact is only at the weekend or every second weekend.

You may be able to convince the judge that it is in the child's best interests to continue to go to the football in your town. By bringing up this matter, however, you are taking a risk. You are alerting the narcissist of something you want, and you can predict he is going to fight you on it. Even if you are successful in getting an order stating the narcissist must take the child to football, he will make the child late for the football each week to push your buttons. He will make the child feel miserable and guilty about going to football instead of spending precious time with him. One thing he certainly will not do is happily follow the judge's order when it has been a specific request of yours. His ego cannot cope with it. The narcissist does not care about the child's wishes or feelings.

You have another option. **By using reverse psychology, you have the best chance to get the positive outcome you seek.** If it benefits the narcissist, he will do it. If it benefits the empath, he will refuse.

If you don't get the positive outcome you seek, you allow the narcissist to *expose his selfish behaviour* to the child himself. It will benefit you a great deal in the future. I understand that this is not a nice thought; to allow your child to see the narcissists true character. No one wants to see their child get disappointed and upset because of an adult's behaviour. However, you need to think of the longer term. What is the best outcome for your child as they grow older? The narcissist is ready to pounce and 'tell on you' to the court if you ever speak one bad word about him to the child. Don't give him the opportunity.

Your alternative to fighting this point in court is as follows;

Don't mention the football to the narcissist or the court during contact negotiations. Don't give the narcissist the heads up. Pretend you don't care about football. When the child has contact, leave it to the child to ask the narcissist to take him to football.

If the narcissist feels that the request is coming from the child and not from the empath, he is much more likely to comply, and take the child to the football. **The narcissist wants to keep the child on 'his' side for his benefit.**

If it doesn't work, don't feel like you have failed. If the narcissist responds to the child by saying;
'No, you are not going to football, you will do the activities I want you to do',
then his behaviour will disappoint the child, and the child sees the narcissist as selfish. You can later console your child and tell them;
'Regrettably, your father won't take you to football. I'm so sorry, but there is nothing I can do about it. During your father's contact, it's his time, and I'm afraid I don't have any power in this situation to change things for you. I can only make decisions about activities during the time you spend with me'.

Your child will see a bit more of the narcissist's true character. You have not exposed that the father is difficult and selfish; the narcissist has exposed it himself, and the child has seen it with their own eyes. It is preparing the child for later years in which, as they become a teenager, they will see and understand more. It's a heart-breaking situation for the child, but it's the reality of the situation in which they are living.

Think of these matters as a win-win situation rather than trying to control small details. You have to let some things go for the greater good. You have to outsmart the narcissist and remain one step ahead. The narcissist, in this situation, will never be able to falsely claim that you have alienated the child because the child will tell the judge what *he* thinks of the narcissist, not what you have taught him to think.

CONTACT DISRUPTIONS

While contact negotiations are in discussion, you already know that the narcissist is going to be late in picking up the child, possibly drop the child late, and quite likely will cancel contact dates or demand a change to a contact date at the last minute and upset your plans. With this knowledge, you can prepare to have the contact order finely tuned to minimise disruptions as much as possible.

If you are using solicitors, then explain to them your concerns, and they can suggest clauses to enter into the contact order to mitigate anticipated problems. Courts often want to see proof of bad behaviour before making orders to stop it. So, consider allowing the narcissist to disrupt the contact at first, documenting it and then at the next court hearing, asking for something to be done about it.

If the narcissist disrupts the contact arrangements, you mustn't let them see that it gets to you. You are smarter!

If your narcissist regularly drops the child home one hour late, you could avoid making plans until a little later, rather than make a big deal about it at court. Choose your battles wisely remember. The narcissist is highly skilled in talking their way out of things like this. It's frustrating. Don't see it as the narcissist winning. You will feel powerful knowing that you are not giving the narcissist the reaction he is seeking. The narcissist never wins!

The child may not mind being dropped home a little late, but as they get older, they might, especially if it starts to disrupt the child's plans. The child will be the one that gets annoyed at the narcissist for continuously messing them about, and the child, once again, sees a bit more of the narcissist's selfish character and bad behaviour. The child will not be annoyed at you. You should not badmouth the narcissist to the child when they disrupt contact. As before, you only remark to the child, it's a shame their father continues to drop them home late, but it's out of your control.

You could try to do something about it at court if the situation is more difficult, and they are continuously disrupting your plans. If this is the case, then send the narcissist a polite email noting the delay and attempting to resolve the matter amicably (example in the next chapter, Communicating with the narcissist). You already know, his behaviour will continue, because you are notifying him of something that is bothering you. Your email is not intent on getting him to stop; it is purely to create evidence for the judge.

The judge may be able to prevent this behaviour in the future by making the contact order more specific. I will give you an example of how to communicate this matter with the judge also later in the book. The judge will be alerted to the narcissist's bad behaviour, which may benefit you in the future. If you do go down this road, then stick to facts and leave out emotions.

Remember - when the child reaches an age of voicing their opinion to the court, then the only loser is going to be the narcissist. You must be patient.

5. COMMUNICATING WITH THE NARCISSIST

When you start communicating with the narcissist, after separation, you will start to see the same patterns of abuse you saw with him in day to day life. The narcissist will use 'charm' at times to attempt to get what he wants and to reel you back into his world. He will use 'manipulation', possibly through the children, using them as pawns in his game. But you hold power now. You have healed, you are stronger and wiser and won't get reeled back into the cycle. Your methods of communication change and you start to stand up to his power and control attempts. You want the narcissist to know you won't stand for it anymore. You want him to know 'you know what he is' and you are on to him!

After leaving him, you may have said things like;

- 'You can't control me now, so get back in your box!'

- 'You need to go to a psychiatrist and get treatment for Narcissistic Personality Disorder.'

- 'You are ill, you have a mental health illness, and the recommendations are that I cut contact with you completely, so that's what I'm going to do – goodbye!'

- 'Im not going to let you turn the children against me, all narcissists do that. I'm going to make sure they know what you are so that they grow up knowing all about narcissistic abuse.'

- 'I am free, healthy, happy, and you will always be a sad and lonely loser.'

It's liberating to leave the narcissist, regain your strength and courage which he had stolen from you and let him know that you are not going to put up with his evil ways anymore. Unfortunately, you are not quite 'free' yet! With litigation hanging over you, the spotlight is going to shine on your communications with the narcissist, for as long as court proceedings take.

The narcissist's inability to communicate with you in a 'reasonable, understanding and co-operative' manner has been extremely difficult in the past and has caused you a lot of stress, frustration and anger. These feelings may have been apparent in your communications with the narcissist while you were with him and since you separated. Now, you are going to be expected to communicate with the narcissist in an 'amicable, non-accusatory, non-judgmental, reasonable' manner. The only problem is, your done with being amicable and reasonable with him, you tried that route for years, it didn't work! He can't see reason; he can't be understanding, he doesn't compromise.

To communicate with the narcissist from now on, in a reasonable, amicable manner, for the sake of the judge, and ultimately for the sake of your child, no matter what the narcissist slings back at you, is a challenge you must accept and face if you want to be successful in your quest to annihilate him.

Using appropriate communication in and out of court is your next major weapon in the war against the narcissist in the courtroom. You might believe you already communicate well. What you believe and what the judge sees are two very different things.

I suggest you communicate with the narcissist by email only so that all conversations are recorded and easily searched. It keeps you sane and helps to avoid heated discussions. It helps keep the narcissist at bay; it stops him from attempting to charm you. It helps prevent losing the information you might need years down the line. Mobile phone communications need to be backed up regularly and generally lead to a quicker response. Occasionally you may respond too quickly then later regret something you said or the way you said it. The narcissist will also *expect* a quicker response from mobile phone, text or messaging application communications. To save the stress, stick to email. Try to use the same subject in the email for certain communications so you can easily find them years down the line, for example; 'Child's education', 'Childs health', Contact arrangements'.

Emails give you time to think carefully about how you word things. How you word your communications with the narcissist is extremely important in this war. It helps to reveal your true nature, and it helps expose the narcissist's character and behaviour. This is your aim!

Keep communications to a minimum and always write calmly and professionally. The more polite your emails are, the more frustrated the narcissist will get and this, in turn, exposes his bad behaviour. For example, when I started limiting my communication with the narcissist, he used to write things in bold, in capitals and in red to demand my attention. It made me laugh, years later, as I explained to a judge how he used to shout at me in emails.

The narcissist will attempt to torment you and get a reaction out of you. He will do it subtly, so it may not appear to others that he is abusive, but you know what he is doing. Don't be manipulated into sending the narcissist an angry and opinionated email in return. **Stick to facts only, don't show emotion** — another weapon in your war.

Remember, the narcissist will be keeping a record as well. You need to behave impeccably. Any deviation from this, and you will find it documented and in court at the next hearing, used as evidence against you, possibly years down the line. Be smart. If you remain calm, it's only a matter of time before the narcissist gets agitated and the mask slips. When it does, all it takes is for him to send you one aggressive, vindictive, angry email for you to have what you need. When he does send this type of communication, don't get mad. Smile and add it to your pile of evidence.

Don't let the narcissist get one grain of evidence from you by letting your emotions get the better of you.

You must use sympathetic language when speaking to the narcissist or you run the risk of coming across as obstructive or vindictive to the judge, and that plays right into the narcissist's hands. It is not an easy thing to do for the empath parent who has undoubtedly suffered from years of abuse at the hands of the narcissist but right now, and in the years ahead, you need to impress the judge. It will benefit you overall in the outcome of your litigation. Remember, the narcissist wants to provoke you; he wants you to be angry and frustrated; it makes him look good. Don't give him the satisfaction. Kill him with kindness instead.

Think to yourself, how would the judge wish to see us speak and behave towards each other, considering we have a child together? (Regardless of what the narcissist has done to you. Remember, the judge's concern is primarily for the welfare of the child.)

Here are some examples of how to improve your communication with the narcissist, to impress the judge;

What not to say (when the narcissist disrupts contact);

EMPATH (to the narcissist, in a frustrated manner): Can you please stop dropping our son off one hour late every Sunday evening? It's making me late for my yoga class every time. I have paid for the session in advance. I know you are doing it to try and disrupt my plans, and I will be sure to let the judge know about your behaviour at the next court hearing.

A better way to communicate this;

EMPATH (to the narcissist in a calm manner): You have been dropping our son off one hour late every Sunday evening. I realise you would like to spend as much time with him as possible, and I know the traffic can be bad sometimes, but I would appreciate if you could try to drop him off on time. He has homework to do on a Sunday evening, and if he comes home late, his dinner is late, and it's difficult to get around to homework before bath time. It just puts our sons routine out a bit. I hope you can consider making the necessary changes to leave a little earlier to cause less disruption to his schedule. It would be greatly appreciated.

How not to respond, when the child is sick;

EMPATH: Our son is not going to school today; he has a tummy bug. I will let you know when he gets better and goes back to school.

NARCISSIST: Thank you for letting me know. Please take our son to the doctor immediately – he must not take time off school without a medical report. Send me the report. Can you please stop letting him take time off school for no reason, it's bad for his education?

You may get angry on reading this response– Who is he to tell you when to take the child to the doctors? You have never allowed the child to take time off school for no reason. What would the judge think if he read that! He is trying to make you look bad to the judge!

EMPATH: I will take the child to the doctor if he needs to go to the doctor, you don't have control of me now, so please stop telling me what to do. As you know, I have never let him stay off school for no reason. Are you taking your medication? Stop telling lies and trying to make yourself look good.

NARCISSIST: Why are you getting so angry at me? I'm only asking you to take him to the doctor when he's ill; I'm worried about him. Take it easy, let me know about the report, thanks

The empath played right into the narcissist's hands. You will learn more about this when I discuss narcissistic projection. Which parent came across as kind, caring and concerned for the child's welfare? The judge would not have been impressed by the empath's response.

A better way to communicate this;

EMPATH: Our son is not going to school today; he has a tummy bug. I will let you know when he gets better and goes back to school.

NARCISSIST: Thank you for letting me know. Please take our son to the doctor immediately – he must not take time off school without a medical report. Send me the report. Can you please stop letting him take time off school for no reason, it's bad for his education?

EMPATH: Thanks for responding, I will monitor his condition, and if he is still unwell tomorrow morning, I shall get him checked out, no problem. The doctor's surgery is very busy, and it is just a minor ailment, I'm sure it's a 24-hour thing and will pass. I will keep you updated. I don't recall a date in which our son had taken time off school when he wasn't unwell, the school report records all absences, and I have informed you each time, on email, when he has been ill.

NARCISSIST: no response

That is a classic example of the narcissist, in the first scenario, coming across as a concerned and caring father, worried about his son's education, and blatantly lying in the email. He portrays the empath as a bad mother but in a subtle manner. In the first scenario, the mother reacts exactly how the narcissist expected her to react. The narcissist came across as caring; the mother came across as angry or bitter.

In the second scenario, the mother's response would have surprised the narcissist and thrown him off guard. He doesn't care if she takes the child to the doctor or not. He wants to exert some control. In this scenario, she comes across as sensible and caring and doing her duty of keeping him updated. The narcissist is exposed.

<u>Communicating a request to remain the resident parent</u>

'Shared contact arrangements, and a residency order with me, has been in place for xxx years. During this time, I have been encouraging and supportive of my child having a meaningful and happy relationship with their father. I am doing my very best to put our relationship difficulties to one side and ensure that contact with both parents is happy and healthy. I understand my ex wants to have residency. These are the reasons I feel it is more beneficial for me to remain the resident parent. (State reasons).

There are some risks to our daughter's routine/wellbeing if residency changes and these risks are xxx.

I hope my ex and I can work towards an amicable relationship with each other, for our daughter to see that we are co-parenting well. There have been several occasions in which my ex has breached orders in the past, and these breaches upset the dynamics of our co-parenting relationship. These breaches are xxx.

I am concerned that if residency transfers, there will be further breaches, and I am concerned that I may not be kept up to date on our child's health, education and wellbeing. If my ex could make positive changes to ensure that orders do not get breached, this would allow us to have a happier co-parenting relationship and set a positive example to our daughter.'

<u>What not to say when negotiating contact arrangements;</u>

EMPATH: During contact, I don't want you to get our daughters ears pierced, please. You know we decided she could get them pierced when she turns ten. I want to stick to this agreement, and have it written in the court order that neither of us will pierce them until she turns ten. Please agree.

The narcissists will respond by taking your daughter to get her ears pierced during the next contact and probably before the ink has dried on the court documents! Or, the narcissist will fight you on it, regardless of what you earlier agreed, and he will ask that she get them pierced at age eight.

A better way to communicate this point with the narcissist is to use reverse psychology, as mentioned earlier;

EMPATH: During contact, we are going to have to give each other a little freedom when it comes to certain things like ear piercing. I know we agreed to get her ears pierced at age ten, but she is asking if she can get it done at age eight now instead. Let us let her, do you agree?

The narcissist will respond by saying;

'NO! We agreed age ten and its sticking at age ten. I will tell the court we have to have it in the contact order that she gets her ears pierced at ten only'.

By making the narcissist think he's in control is one of the smartest things you can do. The narcissist is so predictable that you can use it to your advantage in situations like this. You don't want to be fighting in court over petty things; the judge doesn't have time for it.

The judge will want and expect you to communicate with the co-parent about matters in which both parents should have some say. Remember, judges do not know the complexities of the character with whom they are dealing. **Instead of telling them, show them**.

Very subtle differences in your email communications with the narcissist can make huge differences in the eyes of the court. In the examples of what *to* say, you the empath, appear to be calm, caring and emotionally stable. The narcissist's responses make him look frustrated and controlling. The mission, to annihilate the narcissist, has commenced!

6. COMMUNICATING WITH THE JUDGE

You, as the abused parent, run the risk of talking too much about what the narcissist has done to you in the past and getting too emotional. It's only natural. You have been through a lot of pain at the hands of the narcissist. Courts are not about emotion, though. They are about facts and evidence. The judge is dealing with a lot of very serious matters, and the courts are very busy. Initially, you think that after you have described the domestic abuse, everyone will realise what a loathsome human being the abuser is and you, the kind, caring empath, will be victorious in the court proceedings regarding residence and contact. Just tell the judge he's dealing with a violent, narcissistic abuser and list all his volatile and dangerous outbursts, and that's it surely? Regrettably, this is very different from how family courts operate.

As mentioned earlier, abusers still have parental rights and responsibilities. If you have suffered abuse (which you can prove) and the behaviour is recent, you will likely get protection orders in place. The amount of contact and how the contact will take place is to be decided by the judge if the parents haven't agreed.

If you must communicate with the judge (by way of statement, or affidavit, or answers or even on the witness stand), then the way you communicate will say a lot about your character. Make sure you do this to *your* advantage and the narcissist's detriment. You want to show the judge your true character, the kind and caring empath and not the frustrated, emotional bitter and angry character that the narcissist hopes you will display.

If you are communicating with a Child Welfare Reporter or equivalent reporter from a Child Reporting Agency, then communicate with them as if you were communicating directly to the judge. They are the judge's eyes and ears.

If you are representing yourself, you will have a lot of communications with the judge, and it may be a different judge each time, or it may end up being the same judge that looks at your case each time the orders need to be varied.

Remember, how does the judge want me to behave towards the father of our child? Are my words sympathetic towards the narcissist? Do I appear to be treating him kindly? Be polite, calm, confident and don't swear. (My Lord or My Lady in Scotland, Your Honour in America!)

Here are some examples;

You are trying to get the judge to allow the child to live with you and have supervised contact with the narcissist in a child contact centre. What not to say;

EMPATH to the judge (in a frustrated manner): My Lord, the father was verbally and physically abusive towards me, he's narcissistic, and he goes into a rage at times. I'm worried he's going to go into a rage with the child.

My household now is calm and peaceful. The child should spend more time with me and less time with him. I need supervised contact to take place between the narcissist and the child so that I feel safe in the knowledge my child is safe. He might hurt the child, My Lord, to punish me. He's a violent man.

If he has more time with the child then he's going to turn them against me, I know he is. He's always talking badly about me to the child; he's told them some horrible things about me.

A better way to communicate this to the judge;

EMPATH to the judge (in a calm, compassionate manner): My Lord, I work part-time, and my ex works full time. The child is used to me, waking them up in the morning, making them breakfast and getting them ready for school. The child is used to me, collecting them from school and going home to do homework. The child has had an established routine with me, and it has always worked well. I understand my ex would like to get involved in the child's day to day routine also, but he has to leave the house at 7.30 am to get to work and sometimes doesn't get home till after 6 pm. Therefore, my ex would rely on other family members to step in, whereas I am available, and the child would be happier with no major changes when it comes to the school week.

The child will be able to spend quality time with my ex when they have their weekends together, and they could also spend a Wednesday evening together in which my ex could help the child with their homework.

There have been several incidents in the evening when the child has regrettably seen their father in a rage towards me, and this scared the child. The child cried during these incidents and was confused and upset by their father's actions. I would like to suggest that to make the child feel safe and more comfortable during contact, that supervised contact take place in a child contact centre. It would be in the best interests of the child, My Lord.

<u>You are trying to get the judge to put a specific issue order in place. What not to say;</u>

EMPATH to the judge (in a frustrated manner): My Lord, the father has sent the police to my door on three different occasions under false pretences. He's telling the police that I am not updating him on the child's whereabouts. It's crazy my Lord, he knows fine and well where the child is, he speaks to him on skype all the time. He's trying to control me, My Lord, he controlled me for years, and he's doing it again. He's trying to make me look bad to the police and you. I haven't done anything wrong. He's always done stuff like this, My Lord; he's suffering from mental health illness. I want him to be ordered to stop this behaviour.

JUDGE: (speaking to the father) What's your version of events?

NARCISSIST: Yes, I sent the police. I was worried, she didn't answer the phone for two days. I had no idea where my son was. I miss him so much; I just wanted to know he was safe. I didn't know what to do; I was concerned. I don't get to see my son a lot, My Lord, so when I don't hear from her, it worries me.

Without even realising it, the empath is oozing frustration and making accusations.

The narcissist is, in the judges' eyes, maybe overreacted by sending the police but is a concerned and caring parent.

A better way to communicate this to the judge;

EMPATH *to the judge (in a calm manner): My Lord, we have had the police visit our house three times in the last few years. They seem to be concerned about the child's welfare. The child speaks to his father regularly. When the police came to the house, the child got worried, he thought something bad had happened. The child was confused as to why his father had sent the police. He had spoken to his father the previous day. It's upsetting for the child to have the police come to our house and have all his friends asking him why the police came; it was embarrassing for the child when his friends saw the police car outside. I'm worried about this behaviour, My Lord; I believe an order is necessary for this situation.*

JUDGE: (speaking to the father) What's your version of events?

NARCISSIST: (angrily) I didn't confuse and upset the child, My Lord, it's her fault for not answering the phone, she should have answered, then I wouldn't have to send the police, she's trying to keep him away from me. She needs to tell me every day what my son is doing.

The empath comes across as concerned for the child's best interests (a number one priority for the judge). The narcissist is frustrated that the empath didn't approach the matter in the way he expected her to. He is off guard. His mask slips, and he comes across as being angry, obstructive and controlling.

<u>The narcissist disrupts contact (as described in Chapter Four), and you want something done about it. What not to say to the judge;</u>

EMPATH (to the judge in a frustrated manner); My Lord, the father continuously drops off the child late, every Sunday and it stops me getting to my yoga class on time. He is doing it intentionally, My Lord. He knows I have to leave the house by six pm. He is failing to comply with the court order by dropping him off late, and he needs to know that its wrong and he is not allowed to do that.

A better way to communicate this;

EMPATH (to the judge, in a calm, confident manner): My Lord, there have been some difficulties regarding contact. The child's routine is starting to get disrupted regularly and its starting to upset the child. Please see the evidence submitted of communications between the father and me on these dates. As you will see, I have attempted to resolve matters, regrettably, without success. I believe it's important to comply with court orders, My Lord.

Leave it to the judge to deal with the situation. He may warn the narcissist of the importance of following court orders, and if he does, then the next time the narcissist repeats the behaviour, you have more ammunition. The judge has already warned him so on the next occasion; he might make an order which is detrimental to the narcissist and beneficial to you.

Once again, **subtle differences in the way you communicate make a huge difference to the way the judge views your character.** Your controlled communications with the judge are more likely to cause knee jerk reactions from the narcissist, and this will cast him in a bad light. When you know this, you can tailor all communications to your advantage.

7. THE NARCISSIST'S COMMUNICATION

The narcissist is usually a highly skilful communicator. A narcissist craves adoration, attention, sympathy and regular compliments to inflate their ego. The way they obtain this is through charm, manipulation, coercion and exploitation. They are confident, often cocky, and the court is their platform. It's an opportunity for the narcissist to gain the attention and sympathy he craves and attempts to get a judge as a new best friend. It's also another opportunity to defame your character.

The narcissist will attempt to charm the judge at first, and any other professional involved such as welfare reporters, solicitors, social workers and psychologists, particularly if they are female. If they are male, they will attempt to become buddy-buddy with them.

When the charm doesn't appear to be working then they play the sympathy card;

'Poor me, I miss my child so much, she is keeping her away from me. I want to be a good father!'

'I have parental rights and responsibilities, and she doesn't allow me to speak to the school. How can I help my child and support her at school if she stops me communicating with my child?'

'She tells the child I'm an asshole My Lord, what kind of mother says that about the father? She tells her horrible things about me; I'm so worried about the child and how it will affect her'.

The narcissist methods of communications with *you* in the past, have involved manipulation, guilt, threats and angry outburst. The narcissist communicates emotionally, not logically. Now, however, the narcissist must be on his best behaviour for the court. The mask goes up. He will 'appear' to communicate with you reasonably, but 'reason' is another word that is not in the narcissist's dictionary. He will still be difficult, and still be controlling in his communications but will mask it, in the same way he does face to face in the courtroom – *you* will see through it in his emails, the judge and others may not. Narcissists are masters at this, but once you are onto them, it's easier to spot and easier to respond to, to your advantage.

The narcissist's confidence and charisma allow them to win a war of words against the empath every time. **Do not even consider raising an accusation against the narcissist without hard evidence.** It will result in the narcissist convincing the judge that you are vindictive, manipulative, or the one guilty of the allegations.

The narcissist is always going to be a better communicator than you. You, however, are smarter. **Focus on proving his controlling and abusive behaviour towards the child and exposing his lies.**

He will soon lose his cockiness and charisma, and his false allegations will become his Achilles heel. You are, and always will be, one step ahead, when armed with the knowledge in this book.

The narcissist will most certainly lie during court proceedings. You can guarantee it.

You should never lie in court, court documents or to the narcissist. Lies will come out in court, possibly years later. If you don't lie, you will feel confident that you can answer any unexpected question honestly. Its ammunition for you when the narcissist is dishonest in his communications. If you are well prepared, you can expose the lies. **His lies can ultimately be his downfall.** It might take time, but it's possible. If you can expose your narcissist as a liar, and the lies would have an effect on the outcome of the case, then he becomes an untrustworthy witness in the eyes of the court. You know he is going to do it so it is a huge advantage to you if you can catch him out.

My narcissist got so comfortable lying to the judge over the years; he got away with it so often that in the last official court document he sent, (Official 'answers' to my 'minute') He lied five times in the first page. I couldn't believe my luck. One by one, I provided evidence to expose how each one was untrue. He looked like a fool.

Over time, the narcissist's lies start to unravel, and his true character, bit by bit, gets exposed. By documenting everything and being able to search these documents in the future, you will catch him out in his dishonesty.

The narcissist communicates calmly and confidently while expecting you to continue communicating in the way you have done over recent years. The narcissist does not expect you to suddenly start communicating with him sympathetically, and factually, without emotion. It unsettles him. It triggers him into more hostile communications, and he falls into your trap! Let the narcissist's antagonistic communications contribute to his downfall.

8. LABELLING THE NARCISSIST

When a victim of abuse leaves her partner, she often then analyses his behavioural traits and scours the internet in a search for answers. When the abuser is narcissistic and has several prominent, well-known traits, she may then label the narcissist as having Narcissistic Personality Disorder, along with other mental health illnesses. The victim becomes an expert on her abuser and knows him inside out. When she reads symptoms that match his character to a T, she has no doubt in her mind what her abuser is. She knows his train of thought, his tactics, his manipulation skills and his true self better than he does. Be it a narcissist, a sociopath or a psychopath.

In the case of a narcissist, he does not recognise his behavioural traits as being problematic. He will always be the victim, and the perpetrator will always be you, in his mind, or he will convince professionals that you are equally to blame.

For example, to keep you in the relationship, the narcissist may have agreed to go to a psychiatrist, if you had threatened to leave him. If he went alone for a session though, he would never tell them the psychiatrist the true story of what took place behind closed doors. He would never accept full responsibility for the domestic difficulties. He could convince the psychiatrist that he and his wife are simply having marital problems and that 'both' parties need help to repair the relationship. Gathering troops is another tactical move the narcissist makes to gain sympathy and build up a support network to use against the empath. The length the narcissist will go to, and methods of convincing professionals are one of the hardest things to watch during a litigation process. The narcissist can befriend people easily and manipulate them. Even doctors! It makes it extremely difficult for the empath to get an official diagnosis.

Judges are only interested in facts. They will never accept a medical diagnosis given by the empath and will look poorly upon you for using such terms as narcissist, sociopath and psychopath in the courtroom without evidence. **His skilful deception is one of the narcissists most powerful weapons he will use against you. Therefore, you must not 'label' the narcissist in court** as having any form of mental illness unless you have a formal diagnosis.

If you accuse the narcissist, and you don't have evidence, you are treading on thin ice. Remember, you can't win a war of words against the narcissist. He may even take it one step further and get evidence from an ally to contradict what you are saying. A narcissist can deceive a clinician using charm and convince them into confirming that he does not suffer from a mental health illness. A judge would certainly take note of such evidence. The narcissist would portray you as delusional, accusatory or attempting to smear him.

Don't take this risk. Instead of labelling the narcissist to the judge or other professionals, concentrate on describing his behaviour. Instead of saying 'he is a narcissist and he has bipolar disorder', say 'he displays controlling behaviour towards the child, and his extreme mood swings scare the child'.

9. EVIDENCE, EVIDENCE
& MORE EVIDENCE

After you leave the narcissist, the abuse is likely to continue in one form or another until the narcissist realises that the abuse is being documented and used against him in court. The narcissist will still behave badly, but he will go at great lengths to hide it. Your challenge is to expose this behaviour to the judge.

When the narcissist starts hiding his behaviour, you will find this difficult. You are going to court because you are initiating legal action against the narcissist or he is initiating legal action against you. Most likely, this will involve divorce and or child residence and contact matters. Your case / your defence will no doubt *rely* on evidence of the narcissist's bad behaviour. Now is the time you want him to behave badly; it will support your story. Suddenly, the man who has tormented you for years turns into an angel. Well, in the eyes of the court. You may have been lucky to have already gathered some evidence in the past, but when it comes to court matters, historical evidence can often be irrelevant. So, what do you do?

If you are not already doing so, you must record everything and proactively gather evidence. You maybe be lucky and manage to agree on matters regarding contact through solicitors, or mediation ordered by the court. If, however, matters do not get resolved, a fact-finding hearing or a proof hearing may take place at some point throughout the process. It is a hearing in which you will present your evidence to the judge. (Written and spoken evidence). Whatever the circumstances, when it comes to a narcissist, you cannot start to trust them again, ever! Gathering evidence, even during times of calm, is wise and will keep you one step ahead at all times.

When collecting evidence, keep in mind, what type of evidence is the judge seeking? The judge wants to see evidence from the empath of **how circumstances and behaviour affect the child, not how circumstances and behaviour affect you**.

You may have already learned throughout the healing process that going 'no contact' with the narcissist is the best way forward under normal circumstances. How do you go no contact, however, if he is the father of your children? You are suddenly in this extremely difficult position of having to do so to the best of your ability, without affecting the relationship between the child and the father.

Limit communication to matters regarding the child's health, education, welfare and contact arrangements only. **DO NOT cut the narcissist out of your life completely and restrict his ability to communicate with the child.** This behaviour will be viewed very negatively in the eyes of the judge. Get evidence to show how difficult you find it to communicate with the narcissist about the child so that the judge can understand why you are not attempting to be friends with him for the sake of the child. Judges want to see separated parents being amicable remember, not antagonistic.

(If your circumstances involve criminal behaviours such as serious domestic violence and child abuse then this may be in the hands of the police and or child protection, and you should follow their advice regarding contact and communication with the abuser).

EVIDENCE DURING HANDOVER
Do your best to have a friend or family member present, when handing over the child for contact. The narcissist will use these opportunities to try to get a rise out of you, and then use this against you in court. You need to avoid any heated exchanges with the narcissist, particularly in front of the child. Go into the handover situation calm and prepared. You may need a statement from your witness one day as evidence of any disruptions. Stick to factual communications, say goodbye to the child and leave. Try not to get emotional; remember that is what the narcissist wants. He wants to see your anger, distress and fear. Don't allow it! If there are repeated disruptions during handover, then keep a diary of events.

EVIDENCE OF CLAIMS VERSUS ACTIONS

To counter the narcissist's false allegations and compulsive lies in the courtroom, you are going to need evidence. **You aim to prove how his 'claims' don't match his 'actions'**. If you don't have evidence, create evidence. When I say create evidence, I do not mean falsify. When you study narcissistic behaviour, you learn that you can predict their behaviour. Use the knowledge of being able to predict their behaviour to gather ammunition.

For example;

The narcissists repeatedly 'claims' you deny him contact with his son. But you always adhere to the contact order and deliver the child on time. Your child is always available for telephone calls also.

The narcissist's 'actions', however, have been to reject contact with his son!

When it comes to proving this in court, it may be difficult if you had not documented everything in the early days. The judge might believe the narcissist; he is a very convincing liar. So, what can you do?

You know there will be contact hearings in the future. You are now documenting all the contact dates and times and even have a witness who knows contact had taken place when it was supposed to. You can now prove that his 'claims' are dishonest. But it will be beneficial also to prove that he has rejected contact. You need to prove his 'actions'.

Reverse psychology can work well in this situation. If it benefits the narcissist, he will agree, remember, if it doesn't, he will refuse. We all know the narcissist likes to be in control and doesn't like being told to do anything!

If you offer the narcissist contact at a time which suits you, he is extremely likely to reject it. Do it on email to provide your evidence.

For example;

EMPATH: I have found myself in a difficult situation tomorrow. Someone has gone off sick at work, and I have been asked to cover. My parents are on holiday, and our son mentioned you didn't have plans, would you be able to take our son tomorrow, please? It would help me out, and our son says he would be happy to go and play football with you?

NARCISSIST: No, I am busy tomorrow. You always choose to work, over spending time with our child, be a good mum and spend the day with your child.

A loving, caring father would certainly take additional contact. Only a narcissist will reject it. The child is a pawn to him. He has a connection to the child; he uses the child to supply his need for attention and compliments. Sadly, there is not a bond, mutual love, care or respect.

The narcissist projects onto the empath and makes her feel and appear to be a bad mother. But what the judge is interested in is how the *child* feels. The child was disappointed that his dad had told him he didn't have any plans, and the child felt rejected when the narcissist turned down the opportunity to play football.

I understand you may be thinking;

What if he agreed to the contact? I do not want my child to spend a minute extra with the narcissist if he doesn't have to? That is a choice you have to make in your circumstances.

There were times when my son *wanted* to go for extra contact with the narcissist when there was no legal requirement for him to have the contact. I decided to allow him to. I believe this approach worked in my situation. My son is now a teenager, and I believe he appreciates the fact that I have allowed him to be involved in decisions when it comes to contact with his father. Regrettably, his father did not allow him the same emotional freedom, and that was the narcissist's ultimate downfall.

Not everyone should allow contact out with the contact order. It can result in contact between the child and the father, increasing in the future. It might result in protection orders being affected.

If you don't know what's best in your circumstances, then assess what is most important to you and take legal advice. In my situation, I was fighting repeated allegations of withholding contact, so I believe it was to my advantage that the judge saw the narcissist had additional contact when the child wanted to go. But this approach may not work for everyone.

EVIDENCE TO PREVENT ALIENATION CLAIMS

The narcissist will likely accuse you, in the future, of alienating the child. It happens when the child requests less contact with the narcissist. The narcissist cannot handle such a blow to his ego; he is an outstanding parent in his mind;

'It must be her; she's turning the child against me!'

Don't allow him to get away with these false accusations. He might accuse you, but he won't have any evidence.

Send him regular updates on the child's 'health, education and wellbeing'. Go out of your way to ensure you have a paper trail. If you have a residence order, send the school an email stating;

'I am just writing to confirm that my ex-husband has full parental rights and responsibilities. Please feel free to give him any information that you would give to me, with regards to the child's education and wellbeing at school'.

Sometimes the registration forms for the school mention 'Does the parent have parental rights and responsibilities?' – these forms may be evidence also if you have written 'yes' and can prove that you have put down the father as an emergency contact.

Go out of your way to tell the local doctor surgery too, on email, that the father has parental rights and responsibilities and is entitled to information regarding the child's health and welfare. Save the emails in your evidence folder.

Every time the child is with you, and they get sick or need to pay a visit to the hospital – tell the narcissist, on email, no matter how minor it seems. Title the email 'Health and wellbeing' so you can easily search these emails in years to come.

If you are the resident parent, then the judge doesn't expect you to inform the non-resident parent every time the child has a minor ailment, but if you go out of the way to do it, you are building up your armour against any future attack. The narcissist will probably stop responding to the emails at some point when he realises what you are doing.

You may find that narcissist's respond to emails detailing 'physical' ailments regarding their child, but do not respond to emails detailing 'behavioural' problems. The narcissist cares more about how the child 'looks' than how the child 'feels'.

Proactively sending the narcissist information about the child's health, education and wellbeing could enormously help your defence against any future false allegations. It proves to the judge that you are not vindictive, or bitter and that you include the narcissist in matters involving the child.

You may worry that if you do this, then the narcissist will be disruptive or embarrass you if you give him information about the child's activities, incidents and whereabouts. I found it was useful to tell him slightly after the event, rather than during it!

If you do send the narcissist information and he then acts on that information and causes you embarrassment (to the school or the doctor for example), then apologise for the embarrassment caused (on email) and keep the apology as evidence.

EVIDENCE FROM PROFESSIONALS

A judge will view evidence from a headteacher or a doctor in high regard. Say, the narcissist repeatedly tells the judge you are asking the school not to share with him information about the child. It is a complete lie. You already have your email telling the school the father has parental rights and responsibilities, but you could take it a step further and get an email before the court hearing also.

You could email the headteacher of the school and ask if they would be so kind as to send you an email or a letter, confirming that you have never attempted to prevent the child's father from obtaining information from the school.

This evidence will contradict the narcissist's 'claims' versus your 'actions'.

When the narcissist claims in court one day that you prevent professionals from giving him information and you withhold information, then you have your evidence lined up and ready to counter the false claims. You will have lots of emails to prove that you speak to the narcissist nicely, keep him in the loop about important matters in the child's life and obey contact orders.

ENCOURAGING CONTACT EVIDENCE

You must be seen to be encouraging contact between the child and the narcissist; you must have evidence of this. Consider sending the narcissist an email as follows;

'Dear XXX

Its regrettable contact has not been going so well recently. I hope we can resolve the issues so that happy and healthy contact between you and our son/daughter can take place more peacefully going forward.

Our son/daughter has expressed signs of distress when we are leaving for handover; they cry and fight and say they don't want to go. XXX has witnessed this on numerous occasions recently. Our son/daughter has started being disruptive in school and lashing out. This is unusual behaviour. I hope that we can look at ways to fix this so our child will be content once more.

I feel that there are a few behaviour changes that you could make, which would help our child feel safe, secure and happy during contact. I feel we can't let contact continue in this manner in which it is making our child unsettled. We need some resolution.

Our son/daughter would appreciate it if you would consider allowing them to phone me once for five minutes during the days, they spend with you. It would be reassuring for the child.

Our son/daughter would appreciate it if you would consider taking them to the sports events that they wish to go to some weekends since they prefer to spend time with their friends from their class, rather than with XXX.

It would reassure our son/daughter if you picked them up and dropped them off at times stated in the contact order. Sometimes the child is impatiently waiting, and one time they missed a birthday party when you returned them late. This upset our son/daughter, and they cried for an hour afterwards.

I hope you will consider making these changes to allow for healthier contact in the future. I believe our son/daughter would not get so stressed and emotional when it comes to handover if you took positive action to resolve these issues. Please for the sake of our child. I hope you will think about it.'

The narcissist will flip when he reads the email. He will take it as criticism. He will either send you a kneejerk response, blaming it all on you or, not respond at all. Either way, it doesn't matter. DO NOT get involved in tit for tat emails afterwards. Take his response and put it into your evidence folder.

You already know that there is no way on this earth the narcissist is going to comply with any of your requests. When he doesn't, it's more ammunition for you.

You can always send a final response along the lines of;

'I'm sorry you feel that way, I hope you will reconsider what I have asked'.

Do not feel the need to defend yourself against whatever he throws at you. You can save your defence for the court at a later time. This is purely a mission to get some very specific evidence which will help you in the future.

I know how excruciatingly difficult it is to get your head around the concept of speaking in this manner to the narcissist, but the consequences of being found guilty of parental alienation are severe, so you must have evidence showing that you behave and communicate in a manner that the judge expects of you.

 This is not the behaviour of a parent who manipulates her child and turns them against their father. When he falsely accuses you, you can proudly present your hard evidence in your defence. You will expose his dishonesty.

Other useful evidence;

- A letter or medical report from a doctor or another clinician such as therapist or child psychologist

- Evidence of health issues relating to any pressures of litigation on the child. Evidence of mental health or behavioural issues displayed by the child.

- Did you go to the doctor because the stress of the abusive circumstances was overwhelming for the child and ask the clinician for help?

- Did you go to the doctor because the narcissist was repeatedly taking you to court, causing you extraordinary stress and therefore stress for the child?

- Did you take your child to see a child psychologist? Did you ask them to help you deal with how to co-parent with an abusive ex-partner who you found extremely unreasonable to deal with and who displayed controlling and abusive behaviour towards you and the child?

  (Remember, you are seeking evidence of the effects of the narcissist's behaviour. You do not want evidence showing you are an emotional wreck and can't deal with situations or the narcissist could use it against you and claim you are an unfit mother).

- Photographic evidence of any injuries you have suffered at the hands of the narcissist

- School reports (can show disruption to child's learning/behaviour)

- Did you arrange a meeting with the guidance counsellor at the school to discuss behavioural issues with the child, since the commencement of legal action? Do they have the meeting recorded in the school diary or the child's file?

- Has the narcissist sent any inappropriate communications to the school/doctor/football coach or anyone else, possibly defaming your character? Can you get a copy?

- Diary of events which you have made over time (Not an emotional diary, a factual diary, stating the date, a brief description of what happened, and most importantly, how it affected the child and were there any witnesses)

- Skype/WhatsApp or any other record of communications between child and father

- Police reports – Have you spoken to your local police station because of threats made or carried out by the narcissist?

- Have you asked the police for advice on how the child can be put on the Vulnerable Childs Database so the police will respond to any future call with urgency?

- Has the narcissist shown up at your home in an intimidating manner on numerous occasions and you need the police to give you some advice?

- Did you purchase a rape alarm because the narcissist was threatening and intimidating you?

- Video evidence of the narcissist's behaviour

- Financial records of maintenance payments (or lack of)

- Witness statements from anyone who has seen the narcissist behave in a rude, aggressive or selfish manner, in front of the child. Statements from anyone who has seen the child's emotional state or behaviour caused by the narcissist's behaviour

Note: financial matters do not affect contact in the eyes of the court. If your narcissist doesn't pay child maintenance, then this will not affect the allocated contact he gets with his child, and there is no point raising the issue during a hearing regarding contact. What you can do, however, is use it as evidence to show how the narcissist's *behaviour,* (by not paying it), is detrimental to the child. It affects the child's welfare, and this is not in the child's best interests.

EVIDENCE – COURT DOCUMENTS

Keep all official court documents from each court hearing in a file or online. Don't ever throw away court documents such as minutes, answers, interlocutors, previous evidence, affidavits, statements, welfare reports, judges' opinions. You never know when you will need them in the future.

If you have representation, ask them to make sure you are copied in on all the important official documents. I have used court documents from 2006, in an evidential hearing in 2014. Try to keep them safe.

You will need these if you decide to represent yourself one day and it might not be so easy to recover documents from a solicitor who represented you years earlier.

Having good evidence makes you feel strong, powerful and armed. You will be ready to tackle whatever the narcissist throws at you. You will be in a position to dismantle his lies and expose him.

10.NARCISSISTIC BEHAVIOUR & PROJECTION

You are treading on dangerous ground when going up against a narcissist in court. There is a minefield ahead. You are going to have to step very carefully to get to the other side.

I have already mentioned studying narcissistic behaviour in the healing process. While having a general understanding of narcissistic behaviour is beneficial, there are certain aspects of their behaviour, you must learn about which are crucial when it comes to preparing for court. One thing you can guarantee is that the narcissist is going to behave badly. He is going to mask his bad behaviour for the benefit of the court. Some narcissists can do this better than others. Your mission is to learn everything you can about the behavioural traits he is going to exhibit.

EXPOSING THE NARCISSIST TO THE JUDGE

The narcissist will get well and truly annihilated when his character and behaviour gets fully exposed to the judge. You aim not to tell the judge he's a narcissistic abuser, you aim to *show* him.

There are several ways to do this, and we have touched on some of these in previous chapters. You prove you have the child's best interests at heart, and you prove he doesn't. You prove your good behaviour and prove his bad behaviour. You prove how the narcissist 'claims' differ from their 'actions' and how their allegations towards you, differ from your actions. (As shown in the examples in Chapter Nine). You prove how he lies, how his false accusations are untrue, and you prove his angry outbursts. Most importantly, you prove how all of this behaviour affects the child.

Knowing the narcissist better than he knows himself and being able to predict his next move is imperative for your chances of success.

If you know how they behave, what triggers them and how they react, in advance, you have an opportunity to pull the mask from their face and expose the 'real self' beneath it. You have the opportunity to expose them. You can expose them in the paperwork submitted to the court as evidence on your behalf, or you can expose them in person, in the courtroom itself.

CROSS-EXAMINATION AND THE NARCISSIST
If you have the opportunity to cross-examine the narcissist, you have a chance to expose his behaviour on the witness stand. If the judge sees the narcissists true character and behaviour with their own eyes, this will support your position immensely.

There are certain questions in which you can predict his answers, and by doing so, a well-prepared cross-examination could be his downfall.

For example;

To prove the narcissist is lying

THE EMPATH: Would you describe yourself as an honest person?

THE NARCISSIST: Yes, of course!

THE EMPATH: The following statements are extracts from your answers;

- _The empath consistently disrupts the contact; she is always late_

- _The empath is trying to stop me from communicating with the child's school; I'm not allowed to get school reports_

- _The empath won't let me talk to the child on the phone_

How many of these statements you made, in your written answers, are true?

THE NARCISSIST: It's all true. I'm an honest person!

You then hand the narcissist the evidence you have proving that these statements are not true and exposing his dishonesty. A court relies on facts.

You want him to admit he lied.

To prove their character/bad behaviour

THE EMPATH: Would you consider yourself to be a kind and caring person? During contact, would you say you teach our son skills?

THE NARCISSIST: Yes, yes, of course, I teach him skills!

THE EMPATH: You racially and verbally abused a waitress in a coffee shop, in front of our son two months ago. (You have obtained some proof; you have a witness statement from the waitress. You hand it to the narcissist) *What skills were you teaching our child at this moment?*

You want him to admit his claims differ from his actions.

The narcissist has no evidence to counter yours. You must be careful, though. The narcissist is a skilful communicator and could attempt to talk his way out of the situation and may attempt to draw you into a conversation which you hadn't foreseen. It might be better to go down this path if you have representation. An advocate is also highly skilled at this type of communication and backed with the evidence, will expose the narcissist before the judge's eyes.

By raising the narcissist, by allowing them to boast about their grandiose false-self, and then knocking them with a blow of reality, proving they are dishonest, badly behaved, needy, weak, not as smart as they claim, then you can even trigger their rage right before the judge's eyes.

The cross-examination will certainly cause a narcissistic injury, and when triggered into anger in the courtroom, then the annihilation is well and truly in progress!

EXPOSING THE NARCISSIST TO THE CHILD

The narcissist's inappropriate behaviour, in general, includes lying, manipulation, anger, violence, arrogance, rudeness, selfishness, obstructiveness, vindictiveness and attempts to alienate the child against you. You do not only want to expose these behavioural characteristics to the judge; you also want to expose them to your child. I don't mean you wish to see any ill harm come to your child. What I mean is, rather than *telling* the child over the years what their father is and how badly behaved he is, *you must let them see it with their own eyes*– in the same way, you expose it to the judge. Through your communication, evidence, and bringing the spotlight on their 'claims' versus their and your 'actions'.

You can help prevent the child from being alienated against you by not badmouthing the narcissistic parent to the child. That is what the narcissist wants you to do. Stay one step ahead! Continue to be the kind and caring empath you are. Do not try to compete with the narcissist; show your child through your actions that you are a happy, loving, caring and kind person.

If you open the child's eyes to the narcissistic parent's behaviour, it will work in your favour as the child grows older and 'has a voice' in court. You don't want the child telling the judge or a court-appointed psychologist when he is twelve; 'My mum says my dad is arrogant and selfish because he didn't take me to football'. You want the child to express *their* true feelings, not feelings you have brought them up to feel; 'My dad is arrogant and selfish, he won't take me to football'.

Here is an example of exposing the behaviour to the child;

The narcissist is frequently rude to waiters and waitresses in coffee shops. (The narcissist displays arrogance and feelings of superiority) The child always comes back from contact complaining that the narcissist does this.

It gets you angry; you don't want your child witnessing this inappropriate behaviour, you are worried your child picks up bad habits. You can take the legal route, and at the next contact hearing, explain to the judge and ask for his help. However, we know that the narcissist is convincing and will possibly get away with it, and convince the judge you are petty, and the child didn't understand what was going on. You don't have any evidence; you must not accuse the narcissist without hard evidence. Therefore, a solution in court is unlikely, so what do you do?

You could send the narcissist an email asking that he cease from this behaviour since it is upsetting the child, but, often in these situations, you feel like you may be putting your child in danger, by alerting the narcissist to something the child has told you about them. You don't want the narcissist to get angry at the child for telling you stuff, and you don't want your child to stop talking to you about things they experience with the narcissist and how they feel about it.

You have already learned that if you ask the narcissist to do anything, he will do the opposite unless it benefits him in any way. He does not take instructions from anyone.

It's a very difficult situation for the empath mother to be in, and a situation which becomes a common occurrence, as the child gets older.

You have another option, and that is to let the child witness his father's rude behaviour. When your child tells you about it, explain to your child how you cannot do anything to help him other than teach him to be kind and caring. Teach him it is unkind for anyone to speak condescendingly to another human being. Doing so makes people feel sad, intimidated and embarrassed. Ask him how he thinks the waitress felt in the situation and ask the child how they felt.

Document every time the child tells you of this behaviour and how it affects them. Maybe in the future, you will get some hard evidence of the father's behaviour in front of the child, and then you are armed and ready for the court battle. In the meantime, the narcissist's is exposing his true character to the child. The empath parent is presenting herself as a good role model to the child, and hopefully, friends and extended family of the empath parent will do the same. If the child has loving, good, kind, caring role models all around, who don't talk badly about the narcissistic parent then the child will slowly start to form their own opinions about which people make them feel safe, comfortable and happy and which people make them feel embarrassed, uncertain, upset and confused.

EFFECTS OF NARCISSISTIC BEHAVIOUR ON THE CHILD

Next is one of the most important pieces of information I am going to tell you. **Focus on proving the effects of the narcissist's bad behaviour on the child.** The judge's primary concern in the Civil Family Court is the 'best interests of the child'. It's is a phrase that your narcissist will pick up and use himself countless times in his quest to show the world he is the father of the year. Don't worry about it. *Show* the judge how the narcissist's controlling, and abusive behaviour frightens, confuses, anger's and disrupts the child. **Proving the effects of his behaviour on the child is a very significant weapon in your arsenal**.

Remember the email evidence created;

Email proving that the narcissist had rejected contact with the child – don't tell the judge that the narcissist is a bad parent and how awful he is for rejecting contact. Tell the judge <u>how hurt and disappointed the child was when his father rejected the contact.</u>

Does the narcissist prevent the child from speaking to you during contact? Prove it and <u>explain how this behaviour is confusing for the child.</u>

Does the narcissist display rage in front of the child? Prove it and <u>explain how this behaviour frightens the child</u> (To frighten a child is criminal behaviour in Scotland).

Does the narcissist fail to take the child to the activities they want to go to and instead take them to activities the narcissist wants to do? <u>Prove it and explain how it disappoints and upsets the child.</u>

By focussing your communications to the narcissist and the court, on the effects of the behaviour on the child, you portray yourself as the kind, caring empath you are and expose the narcissist's true selfish, angry and disruptive characteristics. He has nowhere to hide. The annihilation continues!

LYING & VINDICTIVE BEHAVIOUR

Most extreme narcissists in the family court will make false allegations of manipulative, vindictive and abusive behaviour from you, all the traits of which they are guilty. They will attempt to defame your character, publicly humiliate you if they have the opportunity, and will seek custody of children. If they do get custody, they will alienate the child against you.

The narcissist is going to go low in his attempts to make you look bad. You will be shocked by their viciousness, and the skilful manner they communicate these smears to the judge. You will be shocked at their ability to win everyone over and convince them that they are the kind, caring, empath victim in the situation and you, are the emotionally unstable one.

If they know anything that you are embarrassed about or hits a nerve with you (for example you did something you regretted in your student days), then they are going to make it public and use the courtroom as the stage. If it's then written in court documents, they might send the court documents to the school or your work, so that your child's teachers or your boss can read it. They will use it as a reason as to why the child should not be living with you, or how it might affect the child negatively in some way.

The narcissist is not just going to bring up your dirt; he is going to reveal embarrassing information about any family members of yours who may be in your child's life. Possibly something they have done in the past that they regret, maybe even criminal behaviour from their younger days.

I will show you how to counter this. By not allowing the narcissist to 'project' and how you communicate your response to this behaviour is your key to gaining the sympathy of the judge and exposing the narcissist as being troublesome and vindictive.

NARCISSISTIC PROJECTION

The narcissist's ability to project his negative behavioural traits onto you is his number one weapon in this war. Do not allow him to project!

As discussed in chapter one, go back to how you felt when you had recently separated from the narcissist. You are emotionally and physically worn out. The narcissist has left you feeling anxious and unable to make decisions easily for yourself. The narcissist may be attempting to destroy your life, outside of the courtroom. Your mind is weak; you may not have been eating or sleeping properly. You may still fear the narcissist. You can't understand why no one seems to see the narcissist for what he is except you, and this is extremely frustrating.

You are now going to propel into a world where you need to deal with various professionals; You may have to go on the stand and give evidence. Your anxiousness, fear and frustration are going to ooze out of you without you even realising it.

The narcissist has you exactly where they want you. Looking and feeling emotionally unstable. Here is an example of how the narcissist projects;

You know the narcissist suffers from unresolved mental health issues, and you address this in your court documentation, but you don't have any evidence to back it up.

The narcissist says to the judge calmly and confidently;

'My Lord, she has accused me of having mental health issues, but that is untrue, it's regrettable she accuses me of such things, she told the children I'm a psychopath, can you believe it? They were devastated. I've never done anything to deserve this, My Lord. I even have a letter from the Doctor saying I am fine and in good health! She is the one with mental health issues; she went to see a psychiatrist six months ago. I felt so bad for her; she struggled at that time, she was acting erratically, sleeping a lot, not waking the children for school, shouting a lot and scaring the children. I just wanted to help her get better.'

Now, this is a complete lie; and therefore, he has no evidence to back up his story either. The narcissist, however, 'appears' to be emotionally stable. He has his mask firmly in place. The narcissist is crying out for sympathy from the judge while making his false allegations. He is extremely convincing.

You in the meantime, are sitting in the court, absolutely outraged at this accusation, you are in complete shock at how he has lied blatantly and done it in such a convincing manner, you are enraged that the judge looks like he feels sorry for, and believes, the narcissist! You feel the pressure building up inside of you; you can't believe he's getting away with this again! You 'appear' emotionally unstable. You get your chance to speak, and the judge needs to know exactly what your opponent is;

*'That's not true, My Lord! He **has** got mental health problems; he's the one who scares the kids. He was slapping me across the face six months ago, and I just had to go the doctors for a visit because I couldn't take it anymore, he's making it into something that it's not, I can't believe this, he's a compulsive liar!'*

The narcissist looks and acts like an empath, and the empath is accusatory, angry, flustered, and focusing on her relationship with the narcissists, not the effect on the children.

The judge looks sympathetically towards the narcissist, and even your solicitors show signs of sympathy towards him, causing you even more distress. His projection has been successful. He has falsely accused you of suffering from mental health issues, and, the judge who is not completely convinced, since there is no evidence, does wonder whether it may be true.

Here is another example;

The narcissist tells the court that your best friend used to be addicted to painkillers and is clinically depressed. He, therefore, doesn't want the child to be around your her.

You are shocked that he has brought your lovely friend into the court proceedings, you are embarrassed that this information is in court documents that he might make public, and you are angry that he is trying to stop your friend from being around your child.

EMPATH (to the judge, in a hysterical manner) – My Lord I can't believe he's told you that, this is crazy. My friend had a problem years ago; she is fine now. He's doing this to embarrass me, how will I be able to get babysitting help if my friend isn't allowed around the child? This is what he does my lord; he's a nasty person; he's always hated, my friend. He's malicious.

JUDGE (to the narcissist); What's your view?

NARCISSIST (In a calm manner): My Lord, I am extremely concerned about my son, her friend has a house full of pills, and she has had relapses. I don't think it's in the child's best interest to be near her or the pills. It's a dangerous situation to put my son in; he doesn't like being around the friend as he has seen her taking lots of pills in the past. He told me how he was upset by it.

EMPATH: (blows!) That's CRAZY, My Lord, she has NEVER taken pills in front of him, she doesn't have a house full of pills? He's a LIAR, my lord; I can't believe this!

NARCISSIST: I don't know why she is so angry my lord, I only have concern for our child. I don't know why she has to be so nasty to me; I haven't said anything bad about her, my lord.

The narcissist blatantly lies. He projects onto you the traits he is guilty of, (angry and nasty) but he does it skilfully to gain sympathy.

The judge sees your communication towards the narcissist as angry, frustrated and accusatory. The judge sees the narcissist as being caring, concerned, and not talking badly about the empath. The narcissist has successfully projected his negative character traits onto you, and, has successfully masked his true character. The way you 'appear and portray yourself' fits in perfectly with his story.

You now know the narcissist will project and attempt to provoke angry responses from you. He will go for the jugular. **Don't allow him to do this!**

You can throw him off guard by responding to it politely and sympathetically as shown in the communication examples earlier. When he slings mud at you, your calm and sensible response, backed up by solid evidence, is going to impress the judge and make the narcissist look like the troublesome character.

Your aim in the war against the narcissist in court is to show yourself as the kind, caring empath you are (through your behaviour and communication) and expose the narcissist's true character (through his behaviour and communication).

11. THE ANNIHILATION

When you expose the narcissist's true character, it causes a narcissistic injury. Narcissists are deeply troubled human beings; they are full of insecurities and self-loathing. It is why they overcompensate and are often larger than life characters. They lie to themselves, have an over-inflated ego, are completely self-absorbed, and go through life with a huge sense of entitlement. They feel entitled to be emotionally and physically abusive.

The narcissist is incapable of seeing their 'real self'. For example, you or I would look at our mistakes in our behaviour in life and reflect on them and figure out where we could do better. We might think to ourselves 'I judge people too much, and it doesn't make me feel good. I'm going to make an active effort to stop judging people and accept them for who they are'. A narcissist will never do this. They have no faults, in their eyes, they are better than everyone around them, including figures of authority and judges.

So, when you rip the mask off the narcissists face, in public, there are several ways you can predict he will react. The narcissist will explode, retreat or flee. Some of the narcissist's reactions to being exposed are not pleasant, and if you thought you had seen it all, you haven't seen anything until you have triggered a narcissistic injury in a malignant narcissist. The war is not over for them; they may feel they have nothing to lose and display behaviour you couldn't imagine.

When we spoke about cross-examining a narcissist, we touched on how, by building the narcissist up, then giving him a blow to his ego, can trigger a narcissistic injury.

A narcissistic injury can be caused by harshly telling him the truth. It can be caused by doubting him, ridiculing him insulting him and humiliating him. It can be caused by telling him you, and others, can see right through him, you know exactly what he is doing and what his motives are. It can be caused by telling him he is not special; he is just a regular guy, like everyone else or by belittling him and his fabricated achievements. It can be caused by telling him he has done nothing in life worthwhile and has a mediocre job and he is under the control of his boss. You may tell him that he is looking old.

 Unfortunately for the empath, these are all the things you might like to say, but you have the spotlight on your behaviour. You are under the watchful eye of the judge. You cannot risk being mean, cruel and antagonistic.

But another significant way to cause a narcissistic injury is to expose them, and this you can do! You have everything you need.

By going down the route of insulting and humiliating the narcissist, you are more likely to trigger narcissistic rage or an act with a vengeance. By going down the route of exposing the narcissist, you are more likely to trigger their retreat or their disappearance.

Explode;

Narcissistic rage is something to be taken seriously, particularly if your narcissist has been abusive. They may go into a rage, worse than you have ever seen before. They could be destructive and violent. You will never want to trigger this if you are alone with the narcissist or with your children. You will know your narcissist and if this is a possibility for which you need to prepare.

Act with a vengeance;

Vindictive behaviour may follow on from narcissistic rage. The cruel narcissist will attempt to destroy anything you hold dear to you. Your job, your position in the community, your relationship with your friends and family. They may spread vicious rumours about you and will go on a mission to defame your good character. They may send deeply embarrassing emails or messages to your co-workers. If they have any personal photos of you, they may distribute them publicly. (This is also criminal behaviour in Scotland).

Retreat;

You will have experienced 'narcissistic hoovering' in your turbulent relationship, where the narcissist will do all in their power to reel you or the child back into the abusive cycle. It is a significant behavioural trait of the narcissist, which you can predict. If you can predict it, you can prepare yourself for it.

They may go silent for a while, to make you or the child feel guilty. They will then re-appear, weeks or months later, launching the full-blown charm attack, in desperation to reinstate the supply they have lost. The child may get showered in gifts, offers of expensive holidays, false apologies, affectionate messages, and pleading for forgiveness. They will do anything in their power to reinstate the co-dependent relationship, which was once in place. You must be ready for this moment to keep the narcissist at bay.

Disappear;

When you have enough evidence to expose the narcissist fully and completely, they are most likely to flee for the hills. You and your child are no longer narcissistic supply for them. (The narcissist's supply is his insatiable need for love, attention, admiration, affirmation, compliments, which you once, and your child now, provides). The narcissist has no benefit from hanging around after their cover blows, and the mask falls. Their efforts to save face get crushed. The narcissist gets well and truly annihilated!

12.THE CHILD WELFARE REPORT

Judges have several options available to them in deciding what is in the child's best interests and these options are different depending on the court you are attending. The judge may decide themselves, after hearing the child's views, they may order a mediator to assist, or they may order a report get conducted regarding the child's welfare, and this report would give the judge the reporters analysis of the situation and the reporter's recommendations. The judge is not duty-bound to follow the recommendations. The final decision will get made by the judge.

The judge may order a report early on in proceedings, say you have recently separated from a physically abusive partner. The welfare report may be carried out in later years, for example, if the child has been frightened by the narcissist's behaviour during contact or if the child is starting to show signs of waning affections for the narcissist and is starting to reject contact with him.

A Child Welfare Reporter would be appointed to conduct a report in Scotland. The report will take place differently depending on whether it's been a referral from the police or social services, or if the reporter has been appointed directly by a judge. In the case of the

former, the child and the parents will receive a letter beforehand and then will be requested to attend a contact hearing at a Hearing Centre, if required. The child would be asked to fill out a form with some information on how they are feeling. The parents will be asked to give statements. They will have a hearing in front of a panel including the reporter, a social worker, possibly a teacher and three other members, trained volunteers. A 'safeguarder' may be appointed to ensure the child's interests are looked after.
A report shall get sent to the Sheriff, and you will have the right to appeal the decision of the hearing.

CAFCASS (Children and Family Court Advisory and Support Service) would be appointed to conduct the report in England & Wales. NIGALA (NI Guardian Ad Litem Agency) would get appointed in Northern Ireland. In the Republic of Ireland, the Child and Family Agency is TUSLA.

If the welfare report has been ordered directly by a judge in the Court of Session, for example, the report is conducted quite differently. The report would be carried out by an expert witness such as a child psychologist, or by another professional such as an advocate with experience in social work.

Usually, both parents will have one or two interviews, and the child will have one or two interviews, all conducted separately. It can take an hour or two on each occasion and may take place in your home, on the telephone, by skype or in the reporter's office. The child's interview will get conducted in a neutral location, possibly in the school, or a coffee shop, for example, likely in the presence of a teacher. Teachers from the child's school, A new partner in your life, or anyone deemed to have relevance in the circumstances may also get ordered to be interviewed by the reporter.

The report gets sent to both parents and the judge, and a court hearing date gets set for the judge's decision.

It is possible, for the empath to dispute the analysis and recommendations of the welfare report and ask for a further report to be carried out by a different expert. (For example, the first report may have been carried out by an advocate and concluded that you had alienated the child. You may dispute this and request a child psychologist to conduct a report also). You would need to provide sufficient evidence as to the reasons for the dispute.

The judge would then decide which report he found to be correct and which course of action to take thereafter.

In this situation you may be asked to pay for the report split 50/50 with the narcissistic parent and these reports can cost thousands of pounds. I have had one in which the narcissist and I were both asked to send £4000 each in three days as an advance payment.

Needless to say, I nearly fell off my chair, but, the report was an order made by the judge.

It became a choice of paying and continue to fight for my child to get his wishes, which were to make his own decisions regarding contact, or asking the judge to forget the report, in which case my child would have been forced to continue to go for contact against his wishes. The choice seemed a cruel one, and this is the type of twist and turn a court case can take. I have had another welfare report in which the narcissist and I paid around £2000 each and were given around two weeks to make payment.

You will be asked for this money upfront in case either party chooses to walk away from the case. They may even ask you for more than the estimated cost and then refund you the difference.

If a report to assess the child's welfare is ordered by a judge in your situation then, as mentioned earlier, regardless of which agency is carrying out the report, **communicate with the reporter as you would communicate with the judge.** Do not speak badly about the narcissist to the reporter, and, as per communications with the judge, try to keep your relationship with the narcissist out of the discussions and focus on how the narcissist's behaviour affects the child. **You must do this to deflect allegations of parental alienation.**

CHILD PSYCHOLOGIST REPORT
If you feel it would benefit your situation, you can suggest to your representation or the judge that you would like to have a child psychologist conduct the welfare report and state your reasons why you feel it would help the child.

A good reason may be that you feel the report would help identify *behavioural changes* that could take place for contact to continue in a happy and healthy environment going forward. A psychologist might be able to help the child deal with the emotions they have been feeling lately, and the psychologist may suggest ways to improve the child's emotional state.

As children enter adolescence, our parenting style adapts to suit their development stage. A narcissist tends to continue to see a teenager as a young child, whom they must control. A psychology report may determine that the narcissist could make behavioural changes in their parenting skills to adapt to their child's current age.

The psychologist will likely be appointed to determine what the child's emotional state *is* and determine the *child's wishes* regarding contact.

Psychologists study behaviour. You intend to expose the narcissist's behaviour to the judge.

A psychologist's report is an opportunity to expose the narcissist on a professional level. The ultimate annihilation!

Example;
You have followed my advice, and you have behaved well and communicated sympathetically throughout. The child is older now, voicing their opinions more, and starting to get fed up going for contact with the narcissist.

The child is fed up with the narcissists controlling behaviour;

- He prevents the child from using their mobile phone

- He prevents the child from talking to the empath during his contact

- He prevents the child from playing with their friends and insists they play with the narcissist's friends' children

- He wants the child to play rugby, but the child likes football

- He wants the child to cut his hair a certain way, and the child hates it

The psychologist will want to determine how the child is feeling and how any identified behaviour from either parent is affecting the child. The child, on questioning by the psychologist, is likely to tell them of the narcissist's controlling nature and how it makes them feel.

The psychologist is highly skilled at picking up on the child's true feelings and emotional state.

The psychologist will be expected to give recommendations to the judge to assist them in their decision. These recommendations could include behavioural changes that the narcissist could make to make contact with the child a happier and less stressful event for the child.

The narcissist false self is ultimately his downfall. He believes himself to be the best father in the world. When a psychologist suggests behavioural changes, a narcissist could make, to have a happy and healthy relationship with their child, he is highly offended. It causes a significant narcissistic injury. And we know what happens when a narcissistic injury gets triggered!

The narcissist can't accept that their behaviour is the reason for problems during contact. The narcissist will always blame everything on the empath, even when there is a mountain of evidence against them.

A child psychologist may consider 'The Criteria for the Consideration of Contact' when carrying out their report. The primary considerations, holding the welfare of the child as paramount, are;

- What is the purpose of contact?
- Is it safe, physically and psychologically?
- Is it positive for the child?

A psychologist may also look at 'The Risk Framework for the Consideration of Safety of Contact' when carrying out their report. When considering the potential physical or psychological risk involved in direct contact between parent and child, they may refer to criteria put forward by Professor Zeanah (2009) as follows;

Does the parent;

- Accept responsibility for the child's treatment and need to change their behaviour?
- Acknowledge longstanding mental health substance misuse and/or relationship difficulties?
- Demonstrate remorse?
- Place needs of the child ahead of their own?
- Have the capacity for change and have evidenced change in a reasonable timescale?
- Work constructively with involved professionals?
- Make use of available resources?
- Give the child emotional permission to be content in alternative care?

With a narcissist, we already know that 'No' is the answer to these questions, and therefore, direct contact would not be deemed safe until the narcissist has entered into a therapeutic process to change their behaviour. **The psychologist may make this recommendation to the judge.**

There are various outcomes which could take place following a Child Psychology Report.
One of the most important things about taking on a battle in a war against a narcissist in the courtroom is that you cannot predict the outcome.

The narcissist could explode into a rage in front of the psychologist, and the psychologist would then expose the narcissist's behaviour to the court. The judge, who was once captivated by the narcissist, is now enlightened to his true character. The narcissist's armour gets penetrated and the ultimate injury inflicted. The narcissistic father receives criticism of his parenthood by a professional.

Another outcome is that, on receiving the narcissistic injury from the psychologist, the narcissist may retreat for a while in an attempt to gain sympathy from all around. He will appear to be wounded, but he might still feel he has a chance to 'save face' with the court and will grasp on to what he sees as the last chance to regain control over the child, through the psychologist. The narcissist will be incapable of making positive behavioural changes to enhance the relationship with the child. His behavioural traits are already deeply engrained in his core beliefs and values. He will never believe what the psychologist is telling him, but to cling onto his narcissistic supply, he may 'appear' to accept his behaviour needs to change. He may 'appear' to go along with the recommendations and 'appear' to make the changes required, but this will be purely for the benefit of the judge. Once the child reunites with the narcissist, his abusive behavioural patterns will return and continue.

As discussed earlier, another outcome after a narcissistic injury is that the narcissist flees. He realises he is completely exposed and that there is no hope of him grasping onto his supply. He disappears and looks for new narcissistic supply elsewhere.

RISKS OF A PSYCHOLOGIST REPORT
There are risks in going down the path of seeking a psychology report. The psychologist is going to assess and report on your behaviour too. It is common in victims of domestic violence that an abused empath can subconsciously project fear of the narcissist onto the child because of the empaths genuine fear of the narcissist.

For example;
The narcissist has abused the mother but never harmed the child. The mother worries about the child going with the abusive father for contact and warns the child;

'Be careful, if you see your father getting angry then go to a neighbour or call someone.'

The abused empath naturally wants to protect the child and knows of what the violent narcissist is capable. However, she has planted in her child's head that the father is dangerous. The psychologist may say; 'Just because the father has violently abused the mother, it does not mean he is going to exhibit the same behaviour towards the child.'

It is not parental alienation, but it may be considered ammunition for the narcissist.

Another risk is that the narcissist can dupe even a psychologist if the psychologist does not have experience in personality disorders. A narcissist is highly skilled at defending their behaviour by offering highly plausible explanations as to why they did what they did. The charm can work its magic, and the narcissist can gain sympathy from a psychologist, especially if the meetings with the psychologist are limited to only a few hours.

A narcissist can also intimidate a psychologist into becoming an ally in the war. A psychologist will meet a lot of controlling characters in their lifetime. The revengeful narcissist is not one they might like to take on. The psychologist may be so knowledgeable of the character they are dealing with and fear the narcissist's vindictive behaviour themselves. They may fear retaliation, should the report be highly critical of the narcissist. (The narcissist may attempt to defame the character of the psychologist when the court has concluded). It may not be a battle the psychologist is willing to or has time to enter.

Your individual circumstances will determine what your outcome will be. **Assess the situation and decide if a psychology report would be beneficial in your circumstances.**

13.PARENTAL
ALIENATION

One of the most gruelling battles in the war against a narcissist in the family court is when they falsely accuse you of parental alienation.

It's a slap on the face from your controlling abuser when he does this, and then, if he is successful in his allegation and the welfare reporter & judge believes him, it's like a punch in the stomach to the empath. You will be astounded, horrified, humiliated, angry and very emotional.

Parental alienation is the process and the result of psychological manipulation of a child, into showing unwarranted fear, disrespect or hostility towards a parent.

Typically, when an empath separates from a narcissist, the empath is going to make valid claims of emotional or physical abuse by the narcissist, towards her and/or the child. We have learned that the narcissist will get wounded by such accurate claims and will retaliate by projecting their inappropriate behaviour onto the empath. A false claim of parental alienation is an easy option for him. In his mind, the empath is to blame for everything. The narcissist genuinely believes that he has done nothing wrong and that the empath has or will turn the child against him. It is, in fact, something he is more likely to do.

You may have, over the years, displayed some anger at times towards the narcissist and made accusations to him in texts or emails. You may have taken actions to protect your child and to avoid putting your child into a dangerous situation. You may have warned your child of danger, as discussed in the previous chapter. You may have prevented contact at times due to fears that the narcissist will emotionally or physically harm the child.

Your fears and actions are a direct result of the trauma you have encountered and the lack of acceptance and understanding shown thereafter from the narcissist. Your actions are not coming from a vindictive and manipulative place. Your actions are coming from this fear. However, when you are up against such a skilled and callous liar on the battlefield, it makes this deeply personal assault, agonising.

Let's say the child gets to the age of around eight and decides they no longer wish to go for contact with the narcissist. You are going to claim 'abuse', the narcissist is going to claim 'alienation', and the judge is going to have to determine which party is the perpetrator, i.e. the villain. An empath cares what people think about them; an empath cares what the child thinks of them. An empath has self-respect. To be a victim of narcissistic abuse, suffered the torment and trauma that your opponent has subjected you to for years, not seen the narcissist get punished and then have him successfully portray you as the villain is just the proverbial cherry on top of a very poisonous cake. It makes you sick to the stomach. I hope that the insight in this book has awakened you to how the narcissist 'gets away' with such false accusations. I hope you realise what must get done to prevent such allegations, the consequences of which can be unthinkable.

The judge looks at the circumstances presented and must make a very important decision.

Is the child refusing contact with a parent because they are <u>frightened by events which have occurred</u>, or due to <u>feelings the child experiences during contact</u> with the non-resident parent?

Or, is the child refusing contact with a parent <u>because of the negative influence (intentionally or unintentionally) of the resident parent</u>? It may be the case that both are taking place.

If there is a reluctance from the resident parent to help the child move on from the situation and go to contact, even where contact is deemed to be safe, then the parent can be considered to be alienating the child.

Therefore, you must be seen to be encouraging contact in your evidence. I know you are scared to do this, I was too, but the threat of the narcissist gaining more contact time, or gaining a resident parent order, or, having your child taken out of your care altogether is a clear and present danger. You cannot give the narcissist any ammunition which shows you discourage contact.

The situation is more likely to be that the child's continuing reluctance for contact is due to fear he has experienced in the company of the narcissist. The child feels threatened, unsafe, scared to be themselves, controlled and manipulated by the narcissist. The child may have seen the narcissists abusive behaviour towards the mother. The narcissist may have seen a violent outburst from his father. The father may have punished the child inappropriately and disproportionately.

The narcissist parent is unlikely to accept they have been guilty of this behaviour and therefore has not apologised to the child; if they have apologised, it's insincere. The child may, therefore, <u>refuse contact due to the narcissistic parent's inability to acknowledge that they have exposed the child to such distress and the child has no reassurance that circumstances are going to change in the future. The child is genuinely frightened of the narcissist.</u>

The welfare reporter and subsequently the judge has the very difficult task of determining whether the child's reluctance is due to their memories and experiences with the narcissist or the negative influences of the empath or a combination of both.

If you follow the advice in this book, then you will have the evidence for any 'fact-finding' or 'proof' hearing and the narcissist will have none, other than the evidence he has fabricated. You will have the tools to dismantle any false evidence he provides through your solid evidence.

Take allegations of parental alienation seriously and do not allow him to penetrate your armour.

14. THE IMPACT ON THE CHILD

It is without a doubt that litigation between parents has a detrimental effect on the child. Between the age of around three to seven, a child has a basic understanding of what divorce is, and they can sense the animosity between the separated parents. Between the age of eight to fourteen, the child develops an accurate understanding of the root cause of the dispute between their parents.

The severely stressed empath parent, going through court action against her abuser, may not even take a moment to stop and reflect on what the overall impact on the child will be, and, if there is anything that can be done to prevent it.

When you shift your focus from the 'war' to the focus on 'the effects of the war on the child', you can take steps to do your best to mitigate the negative impact the proceedings have on them.

Try your best to avoid talking about court proceedings in front of the child. They hate it.

The child may see the empath parent broken, angry, frustrated, emotional and feeling overwhelmed by all the litigation with the narcissist. It will be hard to hide these emotions at times. It will upset the child to know the parents are fighting each other in court.

The child might have to have numerous meetings with welfare reporters, mediators, clinicians, solicitors and even the judge. The child must open up about their emotions to strangers, prematurely or against their wishes, something which teenagers find hard to do. It can make the child distressed and angry when all they want to do is play on the Xbox or go out with their friends. In some cases, an abusive parent can cross-examine their child, and this is undoubtedly a traumatic event for any child.

Thus, the child's behaviour may deteriorate during times of litigation. It may affect their schoolwork or relationships with friends and siblings.

NEVER attempt to influence the child before a welfare report or a meeting with the judge or any other professional during court proceedings. The narcissist may do this. It will come back to haunt him!

I believe it's important to take your child's views into account when it comes to contact arrangements and to endeavour to follow your child's wishes throughout the entire legal process. The more emphasis on what the child truly wants and the less emphasis on what you want, the better.

In the Scottish court's new legislation in the form of the 'Children's Bill' has recently been proposed to improve the Scottish Family Court system. This bill was vital for child victims of domestic abuse. Under the new legislation, child reporters and child contact centres would get regulated. Reporters would receive domestic abuse training, and this would include coercive control. A parent might not be allowed to represent themselves any longer if there was a vulnerable witness, such as their own child.

In my personal opinion, the Scottish Court system already listened well to the views of the child, but this bill has been designed to put children's voices, views and safety at the heart of decisions made by judges regarding contact after separation. This can only be a good thing for empaths and children affected by narcissistic abuse.

You must relinquish the desire to see the narcissist punished for his behaviour in the civil family court and realign your thought process with that of the family court system.

As young children, they may be perfectly happy to go for contact with the narcissist parent, and they may have a lot of enjoyable moments. And so be it. A child deserves to have both parents in their lives if they wish. Allow them the freedom to love both parents, and when the time comes, the child will decide with which one they want to spend more time. If you attempt to push the child one way or another, you will risk rebellion and the full wrath of the narcissist in court.

The narcissist's punishment comes eventually, and you could say, karma gets him in the end. The more of the narcissist's true character the child sees over the years, the more likely the child is to choose to reduce the contact with the narcissistic parent and want to spend more time with the empath. Rather than force it, try to let it happen naturally. The narcissist will grow old lonely and remain full of self-loathing and unhappiness. You and your child have a chance of abundant happiness in your life.

As they get older, children generally like to have some say in decisions made about their life. As children become young adults, they crave freedom and individuality. The narcissist cannot bear it when the teenager craves control over matters such as how to dress, who they can socialise with, and how much time they spend on Snapchat. The narcissist needs to be in control.

Teenagers reach an age where they are ready to take the reins themselves when it comes to dealing with a controlling parent. Teenagers can be stubborn and can test the waters with the narcissist parent and start to stand up to them. As the child becomes an adult and breaks free from the narcissists control through the court system, they can learn coping skills to help them manage the relationship with the narcissistic parent in the future.

You will be by their side to pass on all your knowledge and wisdom when that time comes!

15.SUMMARY & CONCLUSION

SUMMARY

- Gain emotional stability through the healing process

- Understand how your court works

- Understand the role of the judge

- Choose your battles wisely

- Document everything

- Use appropriate communication

- Ask yourself; 'how would the judge want me to communicate and behave'

- Don't accuse the narcissist if you don't have solid evidence

- Don't label the narcissist

- Be prepared to see his skilful deception and ability to mask his true character

- Be prepared for false allegations of alienation, withholding contact, abusing the child, being a terrible parent

- Record and gather evidence

- Create evidence

- Do not cut the narcissist out of the child's life or prevent the child from communicating with the narcissist

- Be actively seen to encourage contact and have evidence of this

- Remember the narcissist has parental rights and responsibilities

- Do not make unilateral decisions

- Study narcissistic behavioural traits in particular narcissistic projection

- Don't *tell* the judge he's a narcissist, *show* the judge

- Don't allow the narcissist to project his negative behaviour onto you

- Prove your good behaviour and prove his bad behaviour

- Prove how his 'claims' differ from his 'actions' and 'your actions'

- Focus on proving how his bad behaviour affects the child

- Prove you are communicating sympathetically towards the narcissist

- Prove that the narcissist doesn't care about the child's feelings or wishes

- Ask for a psychology report if you feel it would benefit your circumstances

- Never influence/coach the child before welfare interviews or during litigation

- Never badmouth the narcissist parent to the child

- A narcissistic injury can cause the narcissist to explode, act with a vengeance, retreat or disappear

CONCLUSION

When you put this advice into action, you will see the power shift almost immediately. The calmer and more confident you remain, the more unsettled and agitated it makes the narcissist.

The result is you will expose the narcissist's true character and lies, through hard evidence. You will show your true nature and gain the judge's sympathy, something the narcissist craves more than anything.

By limiting discussions of the behaviour of the narcissist towards you, and focussing, on the effects the narcissist's behaviour has on the child, the judge will no longer view you as a possible 'vindictive, bitter ex', and it will support your position as the caring empath with the child's best interests at heart.

You regain control of the courtroom situation. **The narcissist's behaviour becomes their self-destruction.**

The narcissist accuses the empath of the behaviour of which *they* are guilty. If you follow my advice, then the narcissist will not be able to get away with it any longer.

Good luck on your journey. Knowledge truly is power, and I hope you feel armed with insight, which will help you annihilate the narcissist in your life!

I hope you enjoyed my book, How To Annihilate A Narcissist In The Family Court. Please help me to reach other readers by leaving a review on Amazon, or by tagging a friend with a narcissist in their life!

It would be much appreciated.

If you would like to learn more and find other publications, please see my website;

www.rachelwatsonbooks.com

RESOURCES

- SCOTTISH GOVERNMENT website under the Children and Families section. It includes policies on violence and protection against women and girls and child protection. Parenting plan;
  https://www.gov.scot/publications/parenting-plan/

- SCOTTISH COURTS & TRIBUNALS
  https://www.scotcourts.gov.uk/

- SCOTTISH CHILDRENS REPORTER ADMINISTRATION
  https://www.scra.gov.uk/parent_carer/compulsory-supervision-orders/

- CHILDREN AND FAMILY COURT ADVISORY AND SUPPORT SERVICE (CAFCASS, England & Wales) **https://www.cafcass.gov.uk/**

- NORTHERN IRELAND GUARDIAN AD LITEM AGENCY (NIGALA) **https://nigala.hscni.net/**

- DEPARTMENT OF CHILDREN AND YOUTH AFFAIRS (Republic of Ireland)
  https://www.dcya.gov.ie/

- TUSLA (Republic of Ireland) PART OF THE DEPT. FOR CHILDREN AND YOUTH AFFAIRS (DCYA)
  https://www.tusla.ie/services/

- MINISTRY OF JUSTICE
  https://www.justice.gov.uk/courts/procedure-rules

- RELATIONSHIPS SCOTLAND
  https://www.relationships-scotland.org.uk/

- SCOTTISH DOMESTIC ABUSE AND FORCED MARRIAGE HELPLINE **https://sdafmh.org.uk/**

- NATIONAL ASSOCIATION OF CHILD CONTACT CENTRES (NACCC) **https://naccc.org.uk/**

- IYANLA VANZANT: FORGIVENESS **https://amzn.to/2lQkGPO**

- DEEPAK CHOPRA: THE SEVEN SPIRITUAL LAWS OF SUCCESS **https://amzn.to/2m6Y9Oz**

- ECKHART TOLLE BOOKS **https://amzn.to/2kiqS2y**

- RACHEL WATSON: THE NARCISSIST'S BAIT **https://amzn.to/2kHGInw**

- LUNDY BANCROFT: WHY DOES HE DO THAT **https://amzn.to/2lN2F4G**

- SAM VAKNIN: MALIGNANT SELF LOVE NARCISSISM REVISITED **https://amzn.to/2k9tsHU**

Made in the USA
Monee, IL
28 February 2020

22475034R00075